S0-BBY-727

Just the Two of Us

Alicia Blodgett

(c) 1999 by Summit Publishing

All rights reserved. No part of this publication may be reproduced, stored in any retrieval system, or transmitted, in any form or by any means, electronic, mechanical, photocopying, recording or otherwise, without the prior written permission of the copyright owner, except in the case of brief quotations embodied in critical articles and reviews. For information contact:

Summit Publishing
P.O. Box 44
Palm Beach, FL 33480

Published 1999
Summit Publishing
Palm Beach, FL 33480

Designed and produced by Star Group International, Inc.
West Palm Beach, FL 33401

Printed in the United States of America

Library of Congress Cataloging-in-Publication Data pending.

Alicia Blodgett: Just the Two of Us.
ISBN 0 - 9643958-1-9

Revised and updated, Summit Publishing, December 2001
Second Printing, March 2002

Dedications

This book is dedicated to our children:
Billy, Burtt, Shari, Scott, Kurt, and Todd

And to our grandchildren:
Alex, Orianah, Philip, Madeline, Liam, Mercedes, and Marcus

And for all of those not yet born:
That someday when you read this, you will know who we were.

With special thanks to my mother-in-law,
Marcy Cameron, and my father-in-law, Bill Blodgett, Jr.,
for giving me the man of my dreams.

Acknowledgements

I wish to thank my husband, Bill,
for encouraging me to put our story into words.

To Shawn McAllister of Star Group International, for
improving upon those words and inspiring me to write.

To Brenda Star and her staff. It is a pleasure to work with a group of
professionals of such high standards, expertise and ingenuity.

To my mother, Alicia Como, for bringing tons of boat supplies
when she came to visit in exotic places.

And to our cruising friends who allowed me to tell their personal stories.

Table of Contents

1
A Letter to God

It happened like this.

There is a verse in the Bible that says, "All things whatsoever you shall ask in prayer believing, you shall receive." So, I decided to have a heart-to-heart talk with God. You might think I was being bold—and you'd be right—but I figured if God wrote the scripture, I'd hold Him to His promise. After all, what did I have to lose?

"Okay, Lord. I'm ready. I'm ready to give it all to you. I know You are the One who provided for us all these years. You are the One who sent enough so I never missed a house payment. You are the One who made it possible to pay all my bills on time. You have never left us or forsaken us, just like You promised. I'm sorry I turned my back on You, kept You out of my life. But I'm ready now. I know without You, I can't accomplish anything."

This conversation with God took place following seventeen years of an unhappy marriage and six years as a divorced mother. My heart was broken and damaged. I tried. I really tried to make our marriage work and felt like a failure. During those years after our divorce I was spiritually decayed. I felt injured by my ex-husband. How could he abandon his own children, leaving them hurt and confused? I was disillusioned with God. Why did He allow people to get away with bad behavior? But I was guilty of a bad attitude stemming from an aching heart. Yes, I was having a soul emergency.

It took a long time, almost seven years, but one day I realized that even though I turned my back on God, He never left me. God had fulfilled too many miracles in my life to doubt it. A change was coming over me and my heart was alive again. The hurt subsided and I made a conscious decision to give it all to Him.

It's amazing. I'm sure everyone who has carried on a heart-to-heart talk with God understands. Once you surrender, unusual things happen. That's exactly what happened to me.

There were many wrong choices I made and many things I had said or done I wish I could take back. I still do. But God was going to allow me to experience His forgiveness and grace.

"So, Lord, let's get down to the basics . . ." Okay, I wasn't just informal with my heavenly father, I was downright bold. I had resolve and a purpose. You see, my friend Janie Smals called me all excited about how God sent her Mr. Wonderful. She made a list of the attributes she desired and then trusted God to find him. I supposed if it worked for Janie, why not me?

My plea continued, "You know everything, Lord. And now that my heart is healing, I am ready to love again. And I know somewhere out there is a man for me. My mom always said 'there's a lid for every pot,' and I know that You know who he is and that You will bring him into my life. But just in case You need some help, I'm going to tell You exactly what I'm looking for."

Talk about being presumptuous. I not only spelled out my requirements in my prayer, but I wrote them down. Yes, I made a list for God. I started with some pretty serious requests. And it went like this:

1. I want him to be spiritual. I don't mean "religious" because we all know that there are religious hypocrites. I just want him to have a heart towards You.
2. He must be kind and thoughtful of others.
3. He must be highly respected and well liked by others.
4. He should have self-esteem and yet be humble. I know how hard that is. To like yourself but not think too highly of yourself. What a rare quality to find in a person.
5. And, Lord, he must have a good sense of humor. I want to be able to laugh with him. And he should be able to laugh at himself, too.
6. He must have a good disposition and not a bad temper.
7. He must have integrity and be honest and truthful.
8. He must be a faithful husband.
9. He must have strong family values. Please let him like my children. I know it's too much to ask that he love them. It's pretty hard to love teenagers. But if he were just nice to them, I would really appreciate that.
10. He must be fair. You know, if we ever have a difference of opinion—Lord, I hope we never fight—but if we do have a difference of opinion—please let us both be fair.
11. And now, Lord, can I get a little frivolous? I sure would like him to be tall. This one is negotiable, of course. Let's just say the man you choose is short—the important thing is that it does not matter to him.

12. It would be nice if he had a flat tummy. Oh, I know that sounds silly, too. But, wouldn't that mean that he cares about his health?

13. And athletic. You know, I haven't played golf in twenty-five years, since high school. So, I'd like him to be a golfer. It doesn't matter what his handicap is. I'll let You decide. (I just added that to get a smile from You, Lord.)

14. Then again, I haven't played tennis in about ten years. Would it be too much to ask that he is a tennis player, too?

15. And I love to ski. As long as I'm asking, I might as well throw that in.

16. Oh, well, now that I've gone this far, I might as well go for it all . . . windsurfing . . .

17. and scuba . . .

Then as an afterthought, I decided to add the following:

18. Oh, You know, Lord, I've heard that sailors are easygoing people. I think maybe I'd like to do a little sailing.

Perhaps I put a little extra sincerity into this last request or perhaps my pushing the envelope caused God to decide to teach me a lesson. I've often heard you should be careful what you ask for—you may just get it. There's definitely some truth to that statement, because my request to sail would become more prophetic than I expected. In the years ahead, I would often find myself mumbling to God, "Didn't You overdo the sailing just a bit?"

Anyway, that was the end of my primary list. I just had one final, but very important, request remaining.

Now, Lord, the last thing. I don't want to get caught up looking at every eligible man and asking myself if he is the one. Will You please lay it on his heart first that I am the right one for him and then let me know?

As I placed the list in a drawer next to my Bible, I prayed. "There he is. I know it's asking for a lot, Lord. But I also know that if he is out there, You will bring him to me." Janie's plan worked . . . not just for her, but for me as well. Six months later I met the man of my dreams. Bill would be everything I asked for and more.

Actually, the seeds to this meeting were planted about a year before I had my conversation with God. I met Bill's mother first.

My children were begging for a pet. I finally gave in and we went to the animal shelter to adopt a cat. That is where I met my future mother-in-law. Marcy is a very caring lady who volunteers her time every day at the shelter.

Her joy is to make sure the dogs and cats have enough water and are comfortable while efforts are made to find homes for those fit for adoption.

I took to Marcy immediately. There was something special about her. Not only does Marcy want to help animals but she likes to help people, too. Or maybe she wanted to make sure the cat was getting a good home when she asked me the next question.

"Tell me, dear, are you married? No? Well then, what do you do for a living?"

"I sell insurance."

"Oh, wonderful. I need insurance." Can you imagine someone saying—in essence—"I am so happy that I have met an insurance agent." Is that a miracle or what?

The history that brought me to earn my own living was difficult. I didn't share my story with Marcy until long after we got to know each other better. All I told her during this initial encounter was that I sold insurance. But it was a long road I traveled to get there.

In 1982, a year after we were divorced, my ex-husband decided he didn't want to pay alimony or child support. Quietly selling his dental practice, he left the country. This is how I found out.

Early Monday morning, I received a phone call from the receptionist in his office. "Alicia, the doctor didn't come to work today."

I wondered where this conversation was going. "Well?"

"Well, I just found out that he sold his practice to Dr. Smith on Saturday and left on Sunday."

"Left? Left for where?"

"Nobody knows. He's just gone."

How could he leave? He just got married again and bought a house. Why would he leave?

I really didn't have to ask myself that question. I already knew the answer.

He warned me that we wouldn't "get any of his money" and he was true to his word.

When I realized the children and I were on our own, I decided to look for a job as a secretary—the same work I did while he was in dental school. We were married when he was an undergraduate and I never did go back to complete my education. I was told, "Okay, the job is yours. It pays six dollars an hour." With the knowledge that I could never make our house payment on such a small income, I looked in the classifieds to see what the future held for me.

There it was. "Earn $35,000 a year. Will Train. Insurance Adjuster." I can do that.

At the interview I was told, "You don't want to be an insurance adjuster. You can earn more by selling insurance. Why don't you let us train you? Get your license and you'll be out in the field in six weeks. You can make as much as you want and work as hard as you like."

It sounded good to me especially when I thought of my three growing sons at home. We shook hands and I started the next day. And train me they did. Two months later, after going through our savings, I had a license in hand and hit the pavement. It was the beginning of summer in south Florida. A hot one, especially when you have to wear a jacket and skirt and hose, walk through trailer parks and condominiums, knock on doors and "don't forget to smile."

There wasn't time enough to worry about tomorrow. I just concentrated on each day and its problems. Every morning, I would give myself a pep talk. "You love what you are doing." "Today is going to be the best day of your life." And best of all, the message from Paul to the Philippians telling them that we are never alone in this world, "I can do all things through Christ who strengthens me."

I soon discovered being a woman is an asset in a vocation such as sales. People actually opened their doors and were nice to me. Invited me in and listened to my sales pitch. They trusted me. I liked this.

The first day I made $1,200.00. Exactly enough to cover the house payment. That was enough to keep me pumped up and running on empty for the next two weeks. And there were a lot of empty days.

But at the end of every month, our bills were always paid and all our needs were met. We never had more month than money. Beyond doubt God was watching over us.

Marcy's words echoed in my ears. "Oh, wonderful. I need insurance." That's the way every salesman dreams of conducting business. After our animal adoption encounter, Marcy and I kept in touch and she invited me to her home for lunch and to talk about putting together a health plan for her.

Little did I know that what I learned in sales class would be the key to meeting the man of my dreams. We were taught to take special notice of any family photos and start a conversation about what interests people most— their family. On the end table next to my chair was a photograph that caught my eye. I was earnestly interested in the gorgeous man in the picture. So I started a conversation about that one.

"Marcy, who is that man in the photo?" I asked casually, while thinking, "I hope he is her son."

"Oh," she said, "That's my son."

Perfect, I thought. Then continued, "Is he married?"

I felt encouraged to go on when she said he wasn't married, but I was concerned that he looked too young for me. "He looks so young. How old is he?"

"He's your age."

I feared that may not be to my advantage since it seemed most men in their forties want girls in their twenties. I couldn't let it pass. I had to find out. "He's so youthful looking, he probably likes girls a lot younger than he is."

I know I was tipping my hand, but I was genuinely interested and wanted answers more than I was concerned about Marcy's reaction to me personally at this point.

"No, actually he likes women his own age." I began to suspect that Marcy was warming up to playing matchmaker.

As I noticed that he was pictured with a lovely blonde, I said, "Well, I bet he prefers blondes." Since I am a brunette, naturally I had to ask.

"No, he doesn't care what color a woman's hair is."

This man sounds too good to be true. The only thing left for me to find out was how geographically accessible he was.

"Where does he live?"

"In Akron, Ohio."

I knew it. There had to be something wrong with him. Akron is a thousand miles from West Palm Beach, Florida. However, I wanted Marcy to know I was interested in keeping the door open.

So I said, "If he ever comes to visit you, would you introduce us?"

Taking a closer look at me, Marcy responded with "Certainly, dear, I'd be glad to."

Almost a year later my phone rang. "Alicia, this is Marcy. My son is in town. Will you have dinner with us Sunday night? You'll like him. He's tall, handsome and nice."

I had almost forgotten our conversation a year before. I had forgotten what that stranger in the photo looked like. It was the Christmas holidays and I was looking forward to enjoying some leisure time with my children. And Marcy's sales pitch to meet her son sounded too good to be true. But something made me say, "Sure, I'd love to."

"Wonderful, dear. Come to my house about seven and then we'll go to the club for dinner. See you then."

2

The Man Of My Dreams

I'll never forget our first date.

I drove to Marcy's home and rang the doorbell. Oh, well, I thought. It's only one evening out of my life. After all, he's visiting from Akron and I'll never see him again.

Marcy answered the door and Bill was standing a few feet behind her with his movie-star smile. Our eyes met and we shook hands. Following them into the next room, I was introduced to Marcy's friend, Bus Reynolds.

After cocktails and a little conversation, Marcy announced it was time to leave for dinner.

Bill turned to me and said, "Do you mind if we go in two cars? I'll ride with you."

I guess I passed the first test.

"Sure," I said. "Do you want to drive?"

As Bill tried to slide behind the wheel of my old Mercury, I noticed his legs were too long to fit comfortably. Even after he tried to adjust the seat, his knees still touched the wheel. Curious that what I thought was a roomy car didn't fit my long-legged date, I innocently asked him "What kind of a car do you drive?" As soon as I asked I was sorry. I realized it must have sounded shallow. But Bill didn't seem to mind.

"A Chevy Cavalier" was his answer. I couldn't help notice too that he was wearing a plastic Casio watch. Just a regular kind of guy, I thought. Nice, too.

After dinner, Bill suggested that the four of us continue the evening at the Alcazar Lounge in the Breakers Hotel. We listened to the music and danced. Soon, Marcy and Bus said goodnight and we were left there. Just the two of us alone in a crowded room.

Bill and I talked until two in the morning. I couldn't believe what time it was when he told me. It was like the evening stood still. This man could carry on a conversation with a lamp pole. He was fascinating to listen to and Marcy was right ... tall, handsome and nice. The conversation flowed back and forth all evening. I felt I knew him better in one date than the man I had been married to for seventeen years.

We shared likes and dislikes. Hopes and values. The same interests and all the same sports. I was thoroughly charmed and we made plans to see each other the next day.

The following afternoon after lunch, we returned to his mother's house and relaxed for a moment in the living room before going for a walk on the beach. He motioned to me to sit next to him on the sofa. Almost too casually he said, "Do you like to sail?"

I pondered a moment then shrugged my shoulders. "I don't know. I've only been sailing once." I'll never forget the exact words he said next.

"Well," he began slowly. "I like to sail . . . and I've been thinking of retiring and sailing around the world . . . and I was wondering if you would like to go with me . . . but get married first."

At that moment, something happened. Something hard to describe. Something supernatural. It was a confirmation in my spirit and a quiet voice in my heart that said, "This is the one."

I thought about it a whole second and mumbled something like "Yeah." What was going through my mind wasn't the sudden marriage proposal or the invitation to sail around the world, but the realization that this was the man I was going to spend the rest of my life with. It wasn't love at first sight. It wasn't even lust. It was an assurance this was right. Sitting before me was the man God hand-picked just for me.

We just met. We had our first date only twenty hours ago. What in the world could induce two supposedly sane adults to meet and get engaged just like that? Could it possibly be a miracle?

My main concern was pulling up stakes and moving to Akron. I was earning enough to support my boys, but relocating meant forfeiting my residual income and starting over again. I shared my concern with Bill and asked if he would be able to help out financially with my obligations. He smiled. "My mother didn't tell you about me?"

This Chevy-driving, Casio-wearing guy was successful. More than successful actually. I thought he was just a regular, hard-working man. He told me that he worked for a trucking company. He didn't tell me he owned it. He then explained that he sold his business, Roberts Express, to the Roadway holding company but was still the president.

I was stunned. I couldn't help wondering what in the world he wanted with me when he could obviously have any gorgeous young creature his heart desired. I decided to offer him a way out of his offer.

"Are you serious? Do you really want to marry me?"

"Sure," he said. His answer was so straightforward, one would think I had just asked him if he wanted a cup of coffee.

"Do you mean I'll never have to sell insurance again?"

"Not if you don't want to."

Did I want to continue working? Was he kidding? It was that very moment I admitted to myself that I had only been whistling a happy tune to fend away the weight of the world on my shoulders. Sailing around the world would be a piece of cake after the last seven years of single motherhood. Or would it?

The next day Bill asked me if I wanted to go with him to choose a diamond. A diamond. Imagine that. One moment I'm concerned about paying the bills and the next minute I'm sporting a new diamond. I was living out my favorite childhood story of Cinderella.

I let Bill pick out the diamond without me. I was afraid if I chose something too big, he would change his mind about getting married. Or if I chose something too small, I could have opted for something bigger. It's tough being a girl.

I introduced him to my family and friends. They immediately saw in him the qualities I was seeing. My boys, especially, were smitten and thrilled to finally have a dad. Everyone gave us their blessings—even my most skeptical and protective friend, Joanne Pflug.

"Joanne, I met the man I'm going to marry." I could hear skepticism on the other end of the telephone line. "You did? Who is it?"

"Oh, you don't know him. I met him last night."

"What? You're not serious?" She practically leapt through the phone. "This doesn't sound like you at all. I know you better than this. I don't believe it."

"Joanne," I continued, "I know in my heart that this is the man God has for me."

"Before you do anything foolish, I want to meet him." That opportunity came soon and Joanne was won over, too.

We spent all of our available time together that week before Bill flew back to his business. A few weeks later, I followed him to Akron with ten bulging suitcases.

We were married on Bill's 46th birthday, February 9th, 1988. He says I was the best birthday present he could give himself. But I know the truth. He just wants to be sure he never forgets our anniversary.

Life as an Akron housewife agreed with me. Bill would leave each morning about 9:00 and be home by 4:00. We spent leisurely evenings in front of the fireplace, listening to classical music, cuddled up with each other and a good book—growing closer each day. My son Todd came to live with us and finish his senior year of high school. The three of us melded into a happy family and Todd really connected with his new dad.

Every weekend we would drive up to Sandusky on Lake Erie and spend the entire weekend on board *Bodacious*, our Hinckley Bermuda 40. Bill tried to break me in to the sailing life nice and easy. But something else got broken instead.

It was Sunday evening and we were returning from Put-in-Bay, one of the Lake Erie islands, to the marina. It was the first time I had helped dock a boat this size.

Bill showed me how to hold the dock line. He told me to jump off the boat when he brought it to the dock and simply tie the line to the forward cleat. Next, I was to run to the end of the dock and catch the back line and wrap it around the cleat.

I confess. I was nervous. Or maybe petrified is a better word. The thought of jumping off a moving vessel onto a cement wharf was intimidating to me to say the least. I worried that I might land in the freezing cold water and embarrass myself. (I did that six years later in Spain.) Or worse, I might let the boat get scratched.

As though he could read my mind Bill said, "Don't worry about the boat. Whatever you do, don't try to fend the boat off with your hands. We can always get it painted but we can never replace a hand."

When I jumped onto the dock, I twisted my ankle and came down with a thud. I heard a loud crack and knew something was broken. I tried to stand up but the pain was so severe that I had to crawl on my hands and knees to the end of the dock. Bill tossed me the second line as I sat and tied it around the cleat. The boat was safe and sound.

"Are you all right?" Bill asked.

"I don't think so," I said. Bill felt terrible.

We iced the foot and drove back to Akron. I spent the next six weeks in a cast and on crutches. But that's not the worst part. I still had to go sailing for the rest of the summer, plaster cast and all.

About a year after we were married, Bill said, "I have a confession to make. When I asked you to marry me, it wasn't something that I planned to do. Why, I've given more thought in choosing a car. It...it just came out of my mouth...and when it did, my first reaction was 'Who said that?' But then I thought, 'That's not such a bad idea.' And I just want you to know...I'm glad I did."

Was Bill's proposal really divine intervention . . . the work of God? Or was it pure coincidence? All I know is that my prayer was answered. It's hard for me not to believe this was God's doing. Bill responded as though I wrote the script. I believe I did. God cast the roles and brought the scene to life.

He sent me the Man of My Dreams. Bill is everything I asked for . . . and more. I had pushed my luck and asked God for way too many superficial characteristics. I wasn't going to test His patience and ask Him to send someone who was handsome and financially independent as well. Is it any wonder I believe in miracles?

Bill's work kept him traveling during the week and we were seeing less and less of each other. Just as I was getting to know my husband, he was gone. So, I busied myself with decorating a new house, volunteer work and a little tennis. Todd settled into his activities at school. I was relishing my new life. But Bill was working many more hours than he wanted and I didn't realize the travel was dampening his enthusiasm for the executive life.

Two and a half years after we were married, Bill handed me a small piece of paper torn from a sailing magazine with this poem written by an anonymous sailor.

> On an ancient wall in China
> Where a brooding wise man blinks,
> Deeply graven is the message
> It is later than you think.
>
> The clock of life is wound but once
> And no man has the power

To tell just when the hands will stop.
At late or early hour.

Now is all the time you own,
The past a golden link.
Go cruising now my brother
It is later than you think.

"What do you think?" he said. "Are you ready to go sailing?"

I was afraid of this. I knew I promised to sail around the world when he asked me to marry him. But I wasn't ready yet. Not when I was living in a beautiful home. Not when I had all the closet space I ever wanted. I loved my new life. I didn't want to leave Akron. Please, note this. Don't ask me to keep my promise to sail around the world.

3

Sandusky to Savannah

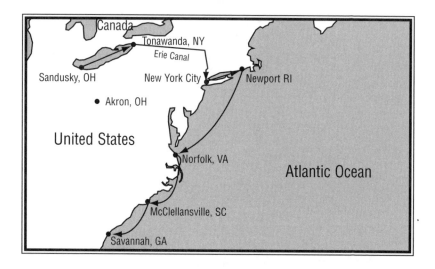

On the morning of Saturday, May 19, 1990, Bill awoke, put on his robe and slippers and walked outside to get the paper. I could hear him yell "Oh, no" even through the thick, brick walls of our house. There in the headlines of the *Akron Beacon Journal* business section was the announcement, "Officer Retiring at 48, Getting Yacht Ready." Bill didn't want to announce why he was retiring from Roadway Services, but somehow word leaked of our plans. Now he felt committed to complete a circumnavigation. After all, it was in the headlines.

The article that followed described Bill's history with the company—how he bought Roberts Express in 1976 when it was a failing local transportation company and turned it into a new breed of trucker that hauled critical shipments. From a Northeast Ohio regional carrier it became a nationwide operation. Roadway bought the company from Bill in 1984 and retained him to run it. In 1988, he was promoted to group vice-president of the holding company and elected a board director.

The article went on to quote Roberts' President Bruce Simpson, "You cannot imagine what a wonderful man Bill Blodgett is. He built this company on the philosophy of shared responsibility and mutual respect." And "Blodgett kept the near-reverential respect of his former Roberts' colleagues after he was promoted to headquarters." There it is. Request number three granted. Well done, God.

As Bill finished his last month of employment at Roadway, I was absorbed in separating a house full of belongings into boxes labeled "store it", "donate it" and "chuck it". Almost every piece of clothing I owned was donated to a shelter for abused women, including the satin negligees I was sure I would never need again. Selling the house and the cars and storing the furniture was the first phase of our circumnavigation.

On July 4th, 1990—the day Bill tagged as our Independence Day— we set sail from Battery Park Marina in Sandusky, Ohio aboard our new 46-foot cutter that Bill insisted on christening *Alicia*. It was the beginning of a remarkable adventure that would last seven years and take us around the world to some of the most exotic places on the earth.

Friends and family were there to cast off the lines. Kurt, my middle son, now twenty, made a special trip from Indiana to help us. Todd, the youngest, was starting another year at Ohio State. There was no joyful anticipation in my heart, only remorse at leaving behind "my babies". As we waved good-bye to our sons, I secretly wondered if we would ever see them again. With a twinge of anguish and a fear of the unknown, I was committed to this and on my way.

Although we were hundreds of miles from the ocean on one of the Great Lakes of North America, those first two days on Lake Erie lulled me into thinking I was sailing the high seas. The weather was clear and sailing was smooth. All I could think about was what a romantic dream we were beginning. Unaware of what lay ahead. I was about to make my first big sailing blunder.

It was just getting dark and time to stop for the night. The warm winds pushed us along under the bright, starry sky.

"Take the helm and steer toward that light straight ahead. Just hold it on course while I go forward to prepare the dock lines," Bill said.

I nervously placed both hands on the cold steel wheel. As the boat tried to swerve, I corrected its movement. Assuming a boat responded the same as a car, I analyzed each slight turn of the wheel. But I soon learned that sometimes a slight turn of the helm would cause the boat to react and other times I had to use all my strength. The response depends on the winds and the current. Determined to keep the boat straight on course, I became intent on understanding this simple, fundamental principle of steering that Bill already knew.

As we kept getting closer to the light, I was resolved to follow Bill's instructions to the letter, but I began to wonder what that light was attached to.

Bill was down on his knees at the bow. I called his name and got no response. The wind caught my voice in the air like a piece of paper and blew it behind me.

I yelled louder but he still couldn't hear me. Looking around, I saw a winch nearby. Grabbing the winch, I clanged it on another piece of metal.

Finally I got his attention and pointed straight ahead. I couldn't see that within seconds we were going to hit the floating cement buoy that was supporting the light. But Bill could.

"Do you want me to keep steering at the light?"

Bill's face registered fear and his eyes grew wide as he scrambled back to the helm. In one swift motion, he grabbed the wheel from my hands and turned it just in time to sail past the buoy.

I burst into tears. "I'm sorry. When you said to steer towards the light, I just did what you asked me to do. You'll never make it around the world alive with someone like me. I'll get us both killed."

With one hand on the helm and a comforting arm around my shoulder, Bill reassured me. "That's all right, dear. You're learning."

That was an understatement. I felt so out of place. Like a bewildered child on the first day of school. Never knowing what to expect next and missing the familiarity and safety of home. So far, this wasn't working for me. The bottom line…I was miserable.

Finally arriving in Tonawanda, New York, we tied up at Wardell's Boat Yard in preparation for our transit of the Erie Canal. The mast had to be lifted out with a crane and placed on the deck because of the many low, fixed bridges.

For nine days we motored across New York State in the narrow canal passing through thirty-five locks. As we approached each individual lock, we would hail the lock operator by sounding three blasts of the horn. This was the signal that we were ready to proceed through. Making certain the fenders were positioned to protect the hull, we waited for the red light to turn green.

Once inside the lock chamber we moved alongside the wall, looping the lines through the rung of a ladder to prepare for what was about to begin. Slowly the gate closed behind us and the water rushed out, pulling us away from the wall. With Bill handling the stern and me at the bow, we quickly passed each line through the rungs and descended. Trying not to let the rope slip from my fingers, I held on tightly while we "locked down".

"Locking up" is much the same except the water rushes in and the boat must be fended off the wall. Taking care to prevent serious injury to hands or feet, we used a paddle to push ourselves away from the slimy wall. Even after locking through thirty-five times, I still did not feel comfortable with my rank of first mate and was relieved to finally reach the end.

Once we reached the Hudson River, it was comforting to have the mast in place again instead of swaying back and forth in the wooden cradles. Celebrating the completion of our first leg, we anchored near West Point and relaxed in the cockpit with dinner by candlelight. The sounds of plebes' voices could be heard going through their freshman rituals as the sun set over the horizon.

Planning to spend time along the coast of Connecticut before embarking upon the trade winds southward to the Caribbean, we had our first of many minor boating calamities when the drive shaft broke in the Long Island Sound and we lost control of the steering. Surrounded by weekend motor yachts, I heard Bill shout, "Steering's gone. We're going to hit another boat. Quick, go forward and drop the anchor."

Who? Me? I thought. I don't know how to do that. I ran forward anyway and stepped on the button as I had seen Bill do so many times before. The little motor that guided the chain up and down—I later learned is called a windlass—allowed the anchor to drop to the bottom. The windlass did all the work, the anchor took hold and I took all the credit. On second thought this isn't so hard. I was beginning to feel like a first mate.

It could have been worse but the only casualty was to our egos. Bill's dad and his wife, Jean, waiting to greet us, couldn't have been too impressed when the boat was left bouncing around in the small channel outside and we had to use our dinghy to row ashore.

We remained in Norwalk several days while Bill learned just one of the many boat repairing skills he would acquire over the coming years. It was strange for me to see my husband with dirty fingernails and sweat rolling off him, instead of coming home from the corporate office in a suit and tie.

At the same time he was learning boat maintenance skills I was learning that the captain is always in command and must be obeyed at all times. Without question. Obedience can be as critical as life or death or as trivial as "hand me that tool". Bill was definitely the captain. If he said to steer to port and I thought we should turn to starboard, I discovered it could be hazardous to question the captain. But Bill was no Captain Ahab. He was a patient teacher. Among cruising couples, one of the biggest complaints is "He yells at me." But not Bill. When the wind was blowing hard or the engines were roaring, I had to ask him to yell.

In the meantime, I was also learning the strange, foreign language that my husband was fluent in. "Sheet in the jib. We're going to jibe" or "Get ready to come about" translated as "Duck!" And that port and starboard thing. It would take me a few seconds longer because I would always have to recite to myself, "Let's see, four letters in left and four letters in port. That means port equals left. Right."

We made a detour up to Newport, Rhode Island to take *Alicia* back to the builder for a few extra comforts since we planned to visit some very remote areas. Alicia was a fine boat to begin with. A floating condominium with two bedrooms and two bathrooms. But a gal needs a hair dryer and a microwave, doesn't she? So that meant installing an inverter to turn DC current into AC current. By the time the water maker (desalinator) and wind generator were added, we felt self-sufficient enough to spend months alone in the most primitive areas of the world.

September was coming to an end and the cold north winds were upon us. It was time to leave Newport for Norfolk, Virginia. This was going to be my first time out of sight of land, our first overnight ocean voyage together and a rite of passage in my new life as a sailor. The trip would take three days and three nights.

The winds were blowing at a brisk twenty knots when we set sail. A light drizzle added to the chill of the air. We slipped into some warm clothing and donned our foul weather gear. I wondered how long I would have to live in this plastic outfit.

After reaching the ocean and starting our course south, we sailed all day in choppy seas and high winds. The weather was rough and I couldn't eat. Just the thought of food made me sick.

Entering the galley, I gripped the counter for balance, head down, aching all over. The thought occurred to me that maybe I'd rather be selling insurance. But, the memory of those long working days brought me back to reality. On second thought, I think I'd rather be seasick.

Without too much enthusiasm, I called up the companionway, "What do you want to eat?"

Bill answered, "Nothing much. I'm not feeling very well."

Thank goodness, I thought with no compassion.

"How about a peanut butter and jelly sandwich?"

"Perfect."

Slapping a lot of peanut butter—a man needs his protein—and a little jelly between two pieces of bread, I tried not to look—afraid I might get sick at the sight of food. Turning my head away, I handed the sandwich up the companionway and felt Bill take it from my hand. Then aching and nauseous, I crawled on my hands and knees to the toilet and retched a little water and a partially dissolved Dramamine. I climbed into the bed and fell fast asleep with exhaustion.

I slept like a baby that first night. Morning came and the sun shone brightly. Well rested but still queasy from the rough seas, I was impressed that Bill was already up and manning the helm.

"Oh, Captain, my Captain," I thought as I gazed at him through misty eyes. Having slept so soundly, I assumed he spent the night down below, next to me. I knew the autopilot could do all the steering, but it never occurred to me that someone had to be on watch to make sure we stayed on course or to "tweak" the sails or, more importantly, to watch out for freighters. Although I didn't know it at the time, Bill was exhausted. I found out much later that he kept an all-night watch, protecting me from much of the reality of sailing, partly because I was sick and partly so the shock of the trip would not change my mind while we were still so close to land.

Once indoctrinated into the real world of sailing, I learned I had to pull my weight and assume a watch. Maintaining close observation at all times is required at sea to ensure your safety and other sailors as well. Watch must be established during any passage. After trying several schedules we found that it suited us better to maintain a night watch of six hours off, six hours on—and a day watch of three hours off and three hours on.

Bill's watch was from eight at night until two in the morning. Then, he would wake me and I would be on duty until eight a.m. After that, I would go back to bed for three hours. This schedule continued until we reached our destination, sometimes as long as several weeks.

A long passage with only two aboard is similar to working the day shift while being married to someone on the night shift. Until your bodies adjust to the schedule, there is hardly any conversation other than "Hello" or "Goodbye." There is nothing romantic about long passages. But once you arrive at your destination, the fun begins and it's worth all the effort.

It was a rough and cold third night. We were chilled through to the bones, even though we were still in our woolies and foul weather gear. Morning brought the first warm day we had seen for weeks. I was delighted that its warmth also brought calm seas and no wind. It meant we were not heeling over and bouncing about and I could use the peace and quiet.

Turning on the engine and entering the Chesapeake, I sat back to relax and enjoy the glistening rays of the sun. But the peace didn't last long when a loud blast of a horn behind us interrupted the quiet of the moment. Looking back, we saw steaming directly toward us a pointed black sea monster appearing to be six stories high. Realizing that we were looking at the conning tower of a submarine and the rest of the ship could be below us any minute, Bill gave way with a hard rudder as the huge ship sped by with several very serious sailors tethered to its conning tower. The headlines flashed through my mind "Unsuspecting Couple Sunk by U.S. Navy."

Is this the way the rest of the trip would be? Someone said that sailing is "hours and hours of boredom, interspersed with moments of sheer terror." So far it was true.

We were glad to be out of the North Atlantic and heading south in the calm waters of the Intracoastal Waterway. The destruction from Hurricane Hugo was constantly visible as we passed towns along the way. We stopped in McClellansville, just north of Charleston on the South Carolina coast, a quaint little place still licking its wounds from Hugo. The damage and devastation were apparent throughout the entire town. Boats were found miles inland and even in trees. Houses were washed away and all the pines destroyed.

The tiny harbor was filled to the brim with large shrimp boats and no room for *Alicia*. While looking for a place to tie up, a shrimper called out and invited us to side-tie next to him. Easing our way over, we tossed our lines and snuggled up next to *Brine Breath*. Even though the shrimp boats were spotlessly clean, the smell of shrimp was strong enough to burn your nostrils. It seemed every shrimp taken from the sea by these men left a permanent memorial.

To reach the dock we had to climb across two shrimp boats and a derelict sailboat left over from Hugo. A hand-written sign on the dock's pay phone advertised "Crab Pot Restaurant. Call and we will come and get you." True to her word, in ten minutes, the owner/waitress/chauffeur was there to pick us up—Mrs. McClellan. Of course, with a name like that you know her roots were deep in McClellansville. She also proved to be a good tour guide as she drove us to the restaurant pointing out the damage caused by Hugo. "Used to be a house there and there and there. All the pines are gone after that 40-foot wall of water hit. Hey, there was even a young couple. Don't know who they were. Jes' passin' through on a little sailboat. Refused to leave the boat 'cause it was the only thing they owned until they got stuck way up in a tree in that boat. Just crawled down out of that tree and ain't never seen 'em since."

She may have just been pulling a couple of strangers legs but nevertheless Mrs. McClellan symbolized all we hear about Southern hospitality. The complete hostess, she prepared and served a delicious meal and drove us back to the docks.

We left McClellansville the next day stopping to play golf along the way. After rounds in Myrtle Beach, Charleston, and Hilton Head, we finally reached our "jumping-off" point, Savannah.

A few days later, we would hit the high seas for a memorable eleven-day passage to the Virgin Islands.

4

Passage to the Virgin Islands

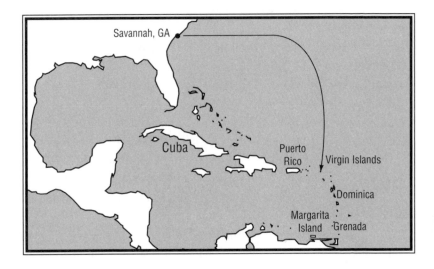

The official end of hurricane season is the first of November. Allowing for a grace period, we left on November 11, 1990. Jumping off from Savannah, we began our 1,500-mile, 11-day trek to the Virgin Islands. Bill was apprehensive about the possibility of a late hurricane or early winter storm. Me? I wasn't nervous. I just didn't know any better.

The big day was cold and we were anxious to get south. Both of us were concerned at the prospect of being so far from land but Bill was looking forward to practicing his sextant skills. Heading due east for 600 miles, we planned to turn right and sail another 600 miles south to St. Thomas. The conditions—choppy and sloppy—were typical of the Atlantic. The waves were short yet steep and coming from every direction. We bounced around like a ping pong ball instead of 15 tons of fiberglass and wood. Pow. We'd get struck on the port side. Slammed on the starboard side. Then we'd do a dolphin motion. The hatches were kept tight because of the seas breaking over the teak deck. Neither of us ate nor slept much and we were sick much of the journey.

This was kind of a starvation diet no one needs. Bill intends to do this for three years? I wondered if I could survive on pretzels and water that long. If not, I would have to call it quits. But did that mean I would lose my husband?

Six days into the passage, I awoke with a terrible feeling of depression and an extraordinary craving for pasta. My hands were shaking. Every cell in my body was screaming for carbohydrates. It was the first time in days that I felt like eating. Standing at the gimbaled stove, I held a pot of water over the gas flame, trying to balance myself and at the same time keep the boiling water from spilling over and burning me. The boat was lurching so much that even the gimbals couldn't keep up with the motion. When the spaghetti was finally cooked, I couldn't get it into my stomach fast enough, shoveling it in my mouth with both hands like some sort of savage.

Almost instantaneously, the depression lifted and the shaking stopped. Later, I learned this was a sign of deprivation that accompanies a reduction of seratonin, a mood elevator. I had a lot to learn about this sailing stuff. From then on, I kept pretzels and raisins in a convenient spot for a quick fix.

When we hadn't seen another boat for more than a week, I became complacent and it almost cost us our lives. It was my watch. Using the binoculars, I scanned the horizon a full 360 degrees for any sign of freighters. Since nothing was in sight, I set the egg timer for twenty minutes and placed it next to me while I dozed, letting the autopilot do all the work. When the alarm went off, I casually looked up. There was nothing ahead of us except white caps. Looking to starboard and port, I saw nothing except more choppy sea. I turned around expecting to see the same nothingness and was startled at what I saw. Not more than 500 yards off our stern a large freighter had just crossed our path.

Knowing what could have happened made me feel weak in the knees. It's no secret among sailors that you should watch out for the freighters. They have been known to sink a small vessel and keep going, never knowing what happened. I vowed to be diligent from then on.

Several years later we learned of such a tragedy. Just off New Zealand, a young mother fell asleep on her watch. A freighter hit them and just kept going. Her husband and two little children perished and she floated to shore on a piece of wreckage several days later. Sadly, stories like this were not uncommon.

We shared watch with four hours on and four hours off, never able to get a full night's sleep the entire time. Hardly a word was spoken between us. How could two people be in such close proximity and yet never have a conversation? How could the words sailing and romantic be used in the same sentence? Was this my husband's fantasy trip?

By the eighth day the seas still weren't calm. I'd had enough and was ready to jump overboard. I plopped my weary body on the settee, partly sitting and partly prone, chin on my chest. Bill assumed a similar position across from me. Raising my head slowly, I looked him in the eyes. Taking a deep breath. I thought, "This is unbearable. How can I tell him I can't go on? Will he ever forgive me?"

As every mutinous thought raced through my mind, Bill returned my gaze. Slowly, he started shaking his head from side to side. Out of his mouth came the words I longed to hear: "I don't like this. We'll quit when we get to St. Thomas."

I was able to say "Okay" quietly, probably because I was too sick to do anything else. In my heart, I wanted to jump up and shout with joy. My spirit lifted with the knowledge that we were going home. I visualized us landing in St. Thomas and immediately heading for the airport, leaving behind the boat and all my new T-shirts that I could gladly do without.

Several times we passed a Navy warship, their helicopters flying over to check us out. Calling to us on the VHF radio channel 16, they wanted to know everything about the captain and crew. Names of all on board. Birthdates. Passport numbers. Boat name. Point of embarkation. Destination. I wondered if they were going to ask what we ate for breakfast. It was reassuring to know they diligently watched out for the welfare of cruisers. So we thought, until a retired Navy man later told us they were looking for evidence of drug smuggling.

Soon, the seas moderated and every sunrise greeted us with the sight of dead flying fish strewn about the deck. It became routine to sacrifice the stiff little carcasses of our unwitting passengers back to the ocean even though some cruisers would eat them.

At last, Bill spoke the words I had longed to hear for eleven days. "I see land." Just a dark spot on the horizon, St. Thomas lay ahead. The excitement of making landfall after a long passage would never wane.

It was Thanksgiving Day and we had a special reason to be thankful. Our first offshore passage and we were right on target. Bill's expertise with the sextant proved successful and I had a very proud husband.

Finally entering the harbor of Charlotte Amalie, we were awestruck by the crystal clear purity of the azure waters. What a contrast between this and the dark, muddy water of the harbors back home.

We eased the boat into the slip and stepped onto the dock. Instantly an abnormal sensation hit both of us. It felt as though the perfectly still dock was rolling and pitching. After becoming accustomed to the storm—tossed sea and earning our "sea legs," now we had to get used to solid ground again. Nobody had warned me about this. I felt dizzy all over again and started to suffer from "land sickness." "Oh, great. What next?" I wondered. "But at least we're going to quit. Leave the boat here and fly home." Or so I thought.

Bill wore the biggest smile I had seen in months. He was on top of the world. Something told me I was in trouble when I saw the pleasure he gained from completing the passage. He walked around the docks lending a helping hand, chatting and laughing with the other cruisers. He was relaxed and cheerful. But I wasn't. Because that was the moment I knew we weren't going home.

5

The Caribbean

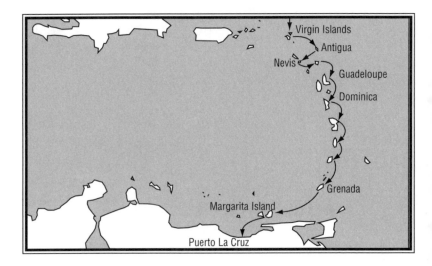

It was easy for Bill to forget the tumultuous passage. He was an experienced sailor and, most of all, an enthusiastic one. Eager for me to overlook the recent rough passage, he did everything possible to try to make me happy. We dined at the best restaurants, went scuba diving at the best spots, and rode on the beach in Antigua. And so we just kept moving along.

Little by little, the cruising life became pleasurable. But the seasickness didn't go away. All I needed was to hear the words, "It's time to leave. Let's raise the anchor" and my stomach would shift into auto-sick. At least now the passages were shorter with only a few hours sail between anchorages.

A first stopover was Tortola in the British Virgin Islands. Even though there was a gentle breeze, it was a hot, sweaty walk to the police station to check in. Taking a book out of my backpack, I sat down on a hard wooden bench and waited while Bill filled out the entry papers.

Officialdom moves very slowly in the islands. No one is in any hurry to cater to an impatient tourist. Often we would sit for hours in a hot, airless office waiting to have our papers stamped and signed.

When the customs official came to the question, "Do you have any guns on board?" Bill answered truthfully that we had a pistol.

The uniformed man approached us as we waited patiently for them to review our answers. "You'll have to return to your yacht and bring us your gun."

"When will we get it back?" Bill asked.

"When you check out."

As we walked the mile back to *Alicia*, Bill explained what was happening. "This means that either we will have to check our gun at each island and spend half a day doing so each time or we'll have to sail back here to retrieve it. That would be a very uncomfortable sail into the wind."

I groaned at the thought. "What's the alternative?"

"We'll just have to skip Bitter End and go straight to the next set of islands."

I was looking forward to Bitter End. Hearing it was a great stop, we didn't want to miss it. "And then? Are we going to have to check the gun each time and go through the hassle of getting it back?"

"Probably."

"What do the other yachties do?"

"Sometimes they just don't declare their firearms."

"But what if we get caught with a gun on board after we check in?"

"We risk the chance of having our boat seized."

"Then let's find a good hiding place for the gun. Anything. Just don't make me sail into the wind for six hours."

From that moment on we carried the gun wrapped in tin foil, stored in an airtight plastic container and hidden in the engine room. We thought this might avoid detection by any gun-sniffing dogs. (Never did meet any of those.) Or any metal-detectors. (Those neither.) Only once during our circumnavigation did we get the gun out. But that's another story told later.

Island-hopping down the Caribbean chain, we stopped at Virgin Gorda, dropping the anchor at Bitter End for a week of windsurfing, snorkeling and eating to our heart's content. I was having fun but granted, after what it took to get here, the playground at McDonald's would seem like fun.

It was the first time in almost three weeks that we heard any news from back home. Every evening we would plop ourselves on the benches in front of the outdoor television and soak up the latest American news on CNN.

Newspaper headlines around the world were flashing "Showdown in the Gulf," "Israel Attacked," "Tense World Awaits War" yet Bill and I were among the few who were unaware of what was happening in the Middle East.

Sitting in the open theater watching a movie, CNN interrupted with a special report on the bombings of Baghdad. One by one the seats filled and soon every guest and employee was there cheering for the United States.

I looked around me and saw the many different faces and races of the world all of them rooting for the good guys and booing Saddam Hussein, shouting "Thank you, America," and "We love Bush." We were unified and yet so diverse. It was a good moment and I was proud to be an American. And to my surprise, I was glad to be cruising so I could have this experience to some-day tell our grandchildren.

Yes, I was beginning the transformation, from land-loving housewife to ship's crew. From having closets full of clothes to only one drawer of T-shirts, one draw of shorts and two pairs of shoes. From monthly beauty parlor visits to chopping my own hair. But worst of all, from a king-size bed to a V berth.

Now please, take a good look at the letter V. That is the size and shape of the bed. Will you kindly tell me how two adults are supposed to sleep in that? Where do my feet go after Bill's size fourteens have claimed their territory? And picture a ceiling only a few feet over your head. Do you honestly think you can get out of this bed without kicking someone in the face?

And can we talk about toilets? Imagine my shock when I discovered I couldn't flush with a flip of the wrist. After all, these are things we take for granted on land. Flushing a head on a sailboat requires strength and practice to do it right. You think I'm kidding? These things come with the instructions on the lid.

First, bend over and grab the handle. Next, pump the handle back and forth to get the water in the bowl. Pump twenty back-breaking times. Then to flush, pump the water out-another twenty back-breaking pumps. Often this needed to be done twice to complete the job. And believe me, you want to complete the job.

Put these two together in the middle of the night—the back flip out of the V and the trip to the head—and you can see it might be hard to get back to sleep after so much activity. It was impossible not to wake Bill when I had to get up. Almost every time he would sleepily inquire, "Where are you going?" I would always respond with more than a touch of sarcasm, "Shopping at Bloomie's."

But Bill kept encouraging me and made cruising life as pleasant as possible, taking on most of the responsibilities. Without much discussion, we separated chores into "blue jobs" and "pink jobs." He took care of all the repairs—autopilot, generator, engine, refrigerator, electronics, windlass, outboard motors, and all the systems constantly needing care. He would navigate, raise, lower and trim the sails and climb the mast. He dealt with the customs and immigration officials.

Among my responsibilities were provision and cook, clean the interior and deck, polish the brass and stainless and the laundry. We shared a few jobs. Changing the oil on *Alicia* was a joint effort. It was Bill's favorite chore and this is why.

Access to the engine was in the galley and no matter how hard we tried, we couldn't do it without spilling dirty oil on the floors, the walls, or us. It had to be timed just right to keep the oil from spraying everywhere as Bill pumped by hand and I switched jugs to collect the warm, gooey black substance. If it got on our clothes they were ruined. After listening to complaints about having to downgrade what few clothes we had to rags, Bill devised the perfect answer to the problem. From then on we changed the oil in the nude. Try that on for romance.

My favorite duty, of course, was that of radio operator. When our trip was still in the planning stages, I earned my ham radio license thinking it would come in handy. And it sure did. Bill installed a ham radio for me and we set up a schedule with my mentor back in Akron. Dave Costello was a priceless friend throughout our circumnavigation. In many locations around the world, when we weren't able to pick up a phone and call home, Dave would be there to patch us in to our family back in the States. How good it was to hear the voices of our mothers in Palm Beach, my sister in Nebraska, or our kids living in California, Virginia, Ohio and North Carolina. It would lift our spirits for days.

Then there was the single side band radio quite unlike the other radios. One day I decided to learn how to use this radio and got out the instruction booklet. Flipping through pages, I discovered that there was something called AT&T high seas service. I could hail an operator back in the United States and make telephone calls that way. The interesting part about it was that while you were waiting you had to listen to other conversations so you would know when it was your turn. It reminded me of the old party line from my childhood. But I think sometimes people forgot that they were "on the air". Some very private matters, best not heard, became pretty common knowledge here.

For instance, this one: The husband was on a yacht somewhere in the Caribbean and his wife was in New York City. His was the first voice I heard and I could picture him on his knees with the phone to his ear.

"Please, Sweetheart, I promise you she is not here with me. It's only us guys."

"I don't believe you, you (bleep). I know she's there and I'm going to divorce your (bleep)."

"Honey, please don't. I promise it's just the fellows here. You don't want to do that. Fly down here and see for yourself."

"Are you kidding? You'd have her out of there before I arrived. I've had it with you. I'm going down to the bank and empty the account and then I'm going straight to my lawyer and take you to the cleaners."

With that, she slammed the phone down and I heard him place the call again.

"High seas operator, I want to make another call." The operator put him through to the wife again and the conversation was pretty much the same. Lots of cursing, allegations of past indiscretions and what she was going to do to get revenge. Then she hung up again.

This time he placed another call to her sister. "Please talk her out of it. She doesn't believe me. I'm not here with another woman. I promise."

"Well, Donald, you know you have a history of this."

"I know, but not this time."

I don't know the outcome of Donald and his wife, but I doubt it was good.

The radio was a great source of entertainment. Another tale we heard is a favorite among cruisers. Some swear it is true. Others say it is folklore. I'll let you decide.

It's a story about a novice sailor who chartered a yacht in the Caribbean and sailed away on a week-long vacation. A while later, he put out a mayday call.

A voice came back saying, "This is the United States Coast Guard to the vessel in distress. What is your emergency, sir?"

His answer was quite unexpected.

"I'm lost."

"Uh, sir, being lost does not represent grave and imminent danger. But if you will switch to channel seven-two, we will be glad to assist you."

Of course, everyone within hearing distance had to follow to channel seventy-two to hear the rest.

"Coast Guard to vessel in distress. Sir, what was your last position?"

There was a long pause.

"I was CEO for The Smith Company."

Another type of radio we had was a VHF. This one is for short range ship-to-shore and ship-to-ship. We soon discovered that the VHF was a good way to stay in touch with other cruisers. Each morning, as soon as we awoke, we would listen to 16, the hailing channel. Here we would "read the traffic" and listen for anyone who might want to call us. Once we got into this routine, we began to make lots of other cruising friends like *Ka Puana*.

"*Alicia, Alicia, Alicia. Ka Puana, Ka Puana.*" Gordon and Joanie Younce were one of the first cruising couples we met. Gordon was a retired Cornell professor. They sold their house, bought the boat and left Newport for the Caribbean. Since their aspirations were also to sail around the world, we thought we found the right cruising companions. Gordon is an avid windsurfer and would zip around for hours with a hook and line trailing behind. He never failed to catch something. Gordon thought the reason he was so successful is because the fish never could figure it out. On one occasion, Gordon came to a dead stop in the water. Something "really big" devoured the fish he hooked only moments before and left him with the top half of an eight-pounder.

Our time together came to an end when they found out that Joanie had cancer. They decided to stay close enough to the States to keep an eye on Joanie's progress. They never did catch up with us and were still there seven years later when we completed our trip. But Joanie was doing fine.

I thought of my oldest son, Scott, celebrating his twenty-fourth birthday back home, as the night of January 20th marked our first painless overnight passage crossing the Anegada Passage to St. Martin. We arrived at Grand Case just as the sun was rising and slipped back to bed to catch up on our sleep.

By the time we awoke it was lunchtime and the aroma of grilled chicken, lobster, and fish filled the air. Walking along the beach where many of the locals turn their yards into restaurants, we selected something delicious to eat, often attracting an uninvited guest…usually in the form of a goat or pig.

Sailing from island to island we visited museums and forts stimulating our interest in the history of the area. Each island has its own distinct flavor and we wanted to taste all we could.

We learned Columbus discovered St. Barthélemy and named it after his brother. The French later settled here, traded it to Sweden in 1784 and bought it back a century later. Most of the natives are descendants of these two cultures. Charming red-roofed bungalows dot the hillsides and there are no high rises or resorts.

The island is a challenge for pilots. As the airport appears over the mountain, a short landing strip abruptly ends in front of the sea. Remnants of small aircraft in the ocean are testimony to the ability needed to land safely. Adding to the danger of landing is a road crossing the top of the mountain. The day we arrived a plane touched down on the roof of a passing car. All in all, I was pleased we arrived in a boat.

Arriving in St. Eustacius we discovered a small, historical island. It is where, in 1776, the first cannon was fired to recognize the new United States of America fleet and caused a war between the Dutch and the English. While diving at the site of one of two hundred and fifty shipwrecks, we found a piece of pottery. After soaking it in vinegar and water to remove the thick crust of coral, the island's small museum identified it as French circa 1700.

St. Kitts, one of the prettiest of the West Indies islands, was next along our Caribbean stops. The high mountains that create much rain here encourage its lush vegetation. The friendly inhabitants greeted us as though we were long lost relatives. Its resident monkeys easily match the island's population of 40,000 people. The green monkey, brought by the French, has lived on the island well over 300 years. We could see them scurry up the sides of the cliffs and hide as we drove by. By slowing down or stopping, we could prompt their curious faces to peek over the hill at us.

Just a few miles from St. Kitts lies its sister island, Nevis, a honeymooner's delight. Although, it doesn't get many tourists since it is a little more difficult to get to and doesn't have a good anchorage for yachts, this was one of our best stops in the Caribbean.

The Four Seasons was completing a luxurious beachside resort with an eighteen-hole golf course on Nevis. We anchored off the resort and took the inflatable dinghy to the dock. As we approached the dining patio, a young lady in uniform greeted us. "Good afternoon. Will you be having lunch with us today?"

Bill responded yes, we would. However, first we wanted to make arrangements to play golf. At the pro shop, we arranged to play a round, and returned to eat. We should have been suspicious that we were dining alone. After all, wasn't this a first-class resort hotel?

The waitress approached without a menu. "What will you have?"

"Could we please see a menu?"

"There is no menu."

"No menu?"

"That's right. Today we have hamburgers or salad."

Bill and I exchanged glances. This is strange for a first-class resort.

"Then I'll have a hamburger and my wife will have a salad, thank you."

The manager came to our table, "I want to explain that the hotel isn't open for business yet. The help is in training. They thought you were visiting management and they were supposed to practice on you. You are welcome to stay here for as long as you like to give the staff experience. At no charge to you. Truly, we would appreciate it because we need the practice on real guests."

"I'm so sorry," Bill said. "We didn't know you weren't open. We just made arrangements to play golf. No one said anything about not being open for business. They just booked us."

"Please, be our guests and enjoy a round of golf on the house. You'll be the first people to play the new course. Just give us a chance to place the cups first. I'll get the grounds keepers started on it while you dine."

And so dine and golf we did. The course was beautiful. The first nine holes curled up the winding hills. At the turn at the top of the hill, the vista was breathtaking with cerulean water and the islands dotting the view. The back nine wound down the hills returning to the resort. The men worked just ahead of us placing the cups and pins in the ground for the first time as we inaugurated the course. The Four Seasons treated us very well for a resort that wasn't prepared to receive customers.

It was here in Nevis where we met local legend Rooster John. We were the only patrons of a little restaurant at a beautiful site at the tip of the island overlooking the Caribbean. A Canadian couple entered and walked right over and asked if they could join us.

"Do you mind if we sit with you? We haven't seen any outsiders lately and it would be nice to converse with somebody new for a change."

During the conversation we learned John and Margaret bought a house in the middle of the main town about 1975 and retired there. They were the first white couple to live in the town and were warmly welcomed.

Soon they became very friendly with their neighbors, all who raised lots of chickens that liked to perch in a mango tree on their property. With so many roosters competing to impress the chickens, the birds would crow all through the night. It began with one rooster crowing to claim his territory. Then the next-door rooster would crow, and on and on all around the town until it came back to their yard and began all over again. With this going on all night they weren't able to sleep.

John tried everything to get rid of the neighbors' roosters. He tried cutting the bottom branches off but they just leaped to the next level of branches. He tried chopping the tree down but only succeeded in breaking his axe on the hard wood.

Frustrated from lack of sleep, John decided to call a meeting with his neighbors to try to convince them to get rid of the roosters. He assumed that these people were experienced in the ways of chickens and knew that their chickens would continue to lay eggs without the roosters' help. The only difference being that the eggs would not be fertilized. Certainly, they could cooperate and get rid of most of the roosters.

Everybody was dressed up in his or her Sunday best. It was a very big occasion to be invited to John's house. The living room was filled to capacity. It was standing room only and punch was served.

After the traditional small talk and a little "warm up" John got to his agenda, "Do the roosters keep you awake at night?"

They all nodded in agreement. "Yeh, mon, they do."

"Then why don't you do something about it?"

"There is nothing we can do about it."

"Well, why don't you get rid of the roosters?"

"Because we want eggs."

"Well," John tried to explain, "you don't need roosters to get eggs."

The look on their faces registered bewilderment. This man doesn't know the facts of life, they were thinking. There was a long silence. Followed by smiles. Then a snicker. Soon the room filled with boisterous laughter. They were still laughing as they walked out shaking their heads. And from then on he was affectionately known as "Rooster John."

Staying at the St. James's Yacht Club in Antigua was a luxurious delight. Anchored in their cove, we were allowed to use all their facilities. We went windsurfing, riding, water-skiing and scuba diving. Bill played tennis every day.

We rode horses across the beach and over the hills. Our guide told us, "You are riding through what used to be farmland, but Antiguans are now farming tourists instead." Tradition in Antigua is that land not farmed can be used by anyone for foraging their livestock. We rode among the goats, sheep, and cows wandering along the countryside.

In Guadeloupe at the little town of Deshais, all that was required to clear customs was to walk up the hill, fill in the forms and leave them in a box. After dealing with so many customs officials at each island, this was a pleasant surprise. Wanting to see more of the island, we hopped on a bus just to see where it would go. Glancing around, I noticed the bus was filled with precious young schoolchildren all wearing their starched blue uniforms, laden with books and well-behaved. All stared back at the two strangers in faded shorts and grease stained T-shirts.

The following day, we sailed over to Iles de Saintes and dinghied to a local seaside restaurant. A four-foot iguana was quietly roaming around the close perimeter of the restaurant. One of the diners near us wanted to capture the beast on film and leaned in to get a close-up shot. The lizard reacted by leaping onto the buffet table full of food. People throughout the restaurant ran for cover. There was chaos. Patrons scurried for safety. Restaurant staff tripped over each other trying to catch the panicked reptile. The iguana made hash out of the cuisine. I never did find out if the fellow who caused the madness ever got his picture.

Our next stop was Dominica. The local fishermen supported themselves as "boat boys." After spotting a sailboat in the distance, they maneuvered their eighteen-foot wooden craft toward the approaching vessel. Sitting at the tip of the bow, they steer by extending their bodies way out to the right or left, moving at a remarkably fast pace in the process. This enables them to keep their hand-held fishing lines in the water while pursuing employment from the newcomers…us. They are as polite as they are aggressive, shouting their name and telling us they will get us fruit or fish, arrange a taxi, tour or laundry. Once arrangements are made with a boat boy, you are his for the duration of your stay and the others bow out. We chose seventeen-year-old Raymond or rather he chose us. Young Raymond was supporting his mother and five brothers and sisters. Just starting his business and not able to afford anything better, he paddled out to *Alicia* standing up on an old surfboard. Raymond took our order for fruit, bread and eggs and was back in a jiffy with our supplies dutifully loaded on his surfboard.

The next day we arranged a tour of Dominica with Raymond's cousin, Alec. Leaving the dinghy on the beach, we hopped in Alec's van and soon found ourselves winding through the mountainous, lush surroundings. He made one quick stop at his home to drop off the fresh fish traded earlier for vegetables from his garden. It was a cute little bungalow he and his brother built themselves. He was very proud that it was paid for and he was currently in the process of helping his brother build one. Alec's mother and sister cared for his three boys while his wife, with the equivalent of an American high school education, taught in the local elementary school.

After hearing warnings about crime in the Caribbean, I asked Alec, "Do you have any serious crime problems here?"

"Not much," he answered. "Punishment is very severe on Dominica. I know a man who got ten years in jail for stealing a gold chain. If you murder someone you are automatically put to death by hanging. With that, we stop and think twice."

Taking a lunch break, we stopped at a garden nirvana on the side of a mountain where the water ran down and formed a little stream. The owner, a Swiss chef, planted a variety of tropical flowers and grew his own herbs used in all his special dishes. Here we were introduced to the delicious soup made from the look-alike elephant ear calalou plant so prevalent in the Caribbean. Hummingbirds buzzed the flowers, the tree frogs sang and the ever-present resident dogs slept at our feet as we ate.

"Now I have a special surprise for you." Alec stopped the van on the narrow dirt road. "Follow that path," he said. "Be careful. It's slippery. But it will lead you to the most beautiful and private place on the earth. I'll wait here until you return."

We entered the tropical utopia of bamboo and ferns and found ourselves in an enchanting rain forest. As we climbed higher, the sound of rushing water grew louder. Minutes later we reached an exquisite waterfall and emerald-colored pool. We were in our own private Eden. Time stood still and I don't know how long we stayed. After a dip, we reclined on the rocks and quietly absorbed the wonders of nature, the sound of the falling water, the diffused sunlight streaming through the tropical vegetation like lace. I could get used to this.

We met many new cruising friends while trekking around the islands. Yachties love to sit around and tell cruising stories. Evening get-togethers for refreshments and story telling became a daily affair. While on board another yacht, the subject of boat boys was brought up.

"I'll never give my laundry to a boat boy again," said Joe.

"Why? What happened?"

"Our boat boy was Roger. He promised us we could have all our laundry cleaned in one day and in time for us to leave the next day. But when the laundry was returned all our underwear and eleven T-shirts were missing. The clothes he did return were dirty. When I asked Roger about the spots on the clothes, his answer was 'Oh, that's jes dirt, Mon'."

"What do you mean 'just dirt'? You were supposed to get these cleaned."

"No, it's not dirty from de wearin'. It's dirty from de dryin'. The woman, she wash it in de river. Then she dries it on de ground. See? It brushes right off."

"Well, Roger, just find the missing laundry and have it back here today. We need to leave soon."

"Yea, Mon, sure Mon. I come bock soon."

That afternoon, Roger returned with the laundry.

"Roger, there are still two T-shirts missing."

"I don't know nothin' 'bout two shirts, Mon. I only know de lady she mad. I jes' git dees shirts and go."

Joe continued his story. "Later that day, a very large local woman was walking toward me on the street wearing my shirt. But she was so big, I knew why Roger didn't want to go back there. I just walked right past her and let her keep the shirt."

Not every island in the Caribbean is beautiful, lush and tropical. Canouan is a dry, brown island and they don't get many tourists. Instead of being besieged by an onslaught of boat boys, we were greeted by a little terrier-type dog that proceeded to follow us everywhere we went. A local lady stopped to chat and we asked her if the dog had an owner.

"Oh, yes, he has an owner," she said. "He's not hungry. He always follows visitors." Since we were the only visitors on the island, he didn't have much choice that day.

We missed having a pet so we encouraged the little fellow to stay near by petting him often. Many cruisers have pets on board but we chose not to because of the inconvenience of having to deal with the animal regulation officials in some countries.

Dogs, cats and even birds were quite common. But we met some strange pets in our travels. One couple in Australia had a pet goose on board. The goose was a clever security system. His loud honk would wake the whole fleet if anyone came near *Stargazer*. That became a problem for Dorothy and Sidney. They were unwanted and the marinas would always be "full" when they radioed ahead for a slip. So to solve their problem, they disguised their voices and fibbed about the name of their boat. It was too late to turn them away when the dock master discovered that it was the couple with the goose arriving.

Another fellow claimed he cruised with a goat.

"One day," he said, "I went to town and left the crew onboard anchored offshore in Papua New Guinea. When I returned to the beach there was a barbecue going. I stopped and bought a plate of meat, ate it and returned to the boat. When I got on board and couldn't find my goat, I asked the men. They confessed they sold him to the vendors on the beach. It took me a minute to take in that I had eaten my pet."

About five miles south of Canouan are Tobago Cays. The contrast between hilly, brown Canouan and Tobago Cays is extreme. Tobago Cays are a group of flat, tiny, deserted islands surrounded by reefs. A national park, they are protected by the government of the Grenadines. The color of the water varies from turquoise to blue to green and the snorkeling is outstanding. The lobster picking was easy here and provided us with a yummy meal.

Then there was Palm Island. When I think of Palm Island, I can still picture the glistening, pink sand and its famous developer, John Caldwell, known throughout the Caribbean as "Coconut Johnny" because he personally planted most of the coconut trees there. John wrote one of my favorite books,

"Desperate Voyage," chronicling his adventures and shipwreck in the Fiji Island of Tuvutha. Ultimately settling down on Prune Island, a mangrove swamp, he promptly changed the name to Palm and also changed the island to a tropical beauty. We ate lunch at the small resort built by John and his wife, Mary, and then sailed one mile to Union Island where another of those small unforgettable happenings occurred...

To get to the customs office at Union, one must walk across the runway of the tiny airport, just a short distance from the anchorage. When we were about halfway across the runway, an official ran towards us, waving his arms and shouting. "Go back. Go back."

We returned to the other side and he stormed over and stood facing us hands on his hips. "You have to wait until the light turns green before you cross the runway." he bellowed.

"I beg your pardon," Bill said.

"Where are you from?" said the official.

Wanting to make it simple and assuming he didn't know where Akron, Ohio was I answered, "Cleveland."

"So, don't they teach you how to walk across the runway in Cleveland?"

Under the circumstances and considering this man was still angry, we decided it would be better not to laugh. How does one explain? We were only getting a small taste of the many cultural differences we would experience in the next seven years. Some of those differences were not going to be as humorous.

It was a short sail to Grenada where we tied up at the Spice Island Marina. With the aromas of nutmeg, vanilla, and cinnamon filling the air, the island seemed to beckon us. So renting a car, we gave ourselves the tour. Along the way, Bill stopped to pick up a couple of young men hitchhiking home from work. "You from America?" one asked.

"That's right," answered Bill. Their eyes lit up.

"We love America. Thank God for U.S." they said. "The U.S. liberated Grenada."

During our trip, wherever we would go, people would have strong opinions about Americans. It was usually very positive, sometimes very negative, but never in between.

I did some reflecting as we prepared to leave the Caribbean and enter Venezuelan waters. For the most part, the islanders were friendly, happy and helpful. They were educated with the equivalent of a high school degree or better, even the boat boys. Everybody seemed eager to help and we never saw anyone begging or homeless.

One thing that always seemed to put a smile on our faces was the abundance of sheep, goats and chickens. They walked the streets and crossed the roads like any pedestrian. Animals were accepted as part of the population. Cows and donkeys would often be seen tethered and grazing by the roads and main highways. Almost all of the restaurants were open-aired with the obligatory dog and cat in residence. Birds would come to your table and eat out of your hand.

One of the most enduring memories from the islands stems from the sounds of the steel band. The music of these bands seems to be everywhere. Any note can be played and they offered a variety of selections. Melodies ranging from country western and popular music to the island reggae permeated the atmosphere day and night, leaving a unique, lasting impression. I could hear Harry Belafonte singing "Jamaica Farewell" in the recesses of my memory bank. The Caribbean is a place in which cruising dreams are born and fantasies become real.

6

Venezuela to The Panama Canal

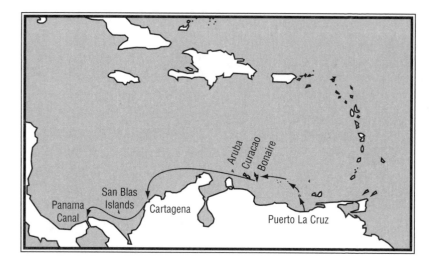

Venezuela's Margarita Island is only a twenty-four hour sail from Grenada but worlds away in its culture.

Two rugged custom's officials were waiting for us as we anchored off shore at Pampatar. Bill rowed in and brought them back to the boat so they could inspect it. The instant they boarded, the burly men began to search inside cabinets. It soon became apparent they were looking for liquor and Playboy magazines. When they realized we had no reading material to interest them, they shifted their attention to our videos.

Pointing to a video that was labeled "EXCEL" they became very enthusiastic. Not speaking English, they were misled by the "X" in the title. Motioning to Bill to play it for them, they sat down and waited expectantly for what they thought was an X-rated movie. When they discovered that they were going to learn a new software program and get no thrills, they hastily stamped our passports and motioned to take them back to shore.

When we arrived at the little fishing village, there were already twenty cruising boats anchored. Small rolling waves continuously lashed into the tiny port, causing a very uncomfortable anchorage. As a result everyone put out a second anchor at the stern in the direction of the waves. At least we would not be rolling from side to side. Instead we rolled constantly from bow to stern. Sleeping at night with the gentle rocking was pleasant, but that same rocking kept us off the boat during the day. In spite of the waves, we stayed three months.

A diverse group of cruisers gathered here, ten degrees above the equator, as a refuge from hurricanes. One of the strangest characters we met in our travels was in Pampatar.

A retired British Navy man, Ronald was of average size, lean and weather-beaten. His boat was a sloop, 35 feet long. It too was pretty weather-beaten. He seemed sociable. He would stop to chat, but there was a certain angry quality in his face. You could tell he was not a man at peace with himself. We soon discovered why.

Ronald just crossed the Atlantic from the Canary Islands. He claimed he had buried his wife at sea during the long passage. True, it's common to put a dead body overboard because most countries won't allow you to land with one of those aboard. But what should be a very sad event didn't seem to bother Ronald at all. In fact, he seemed very pleased about the whole affair. So pleased that his report sounded more like boasting rather than grief.

Perhaps Ronald's stiff-upper-lip manner was misunderstood, but nevertheless, the fleet began to avoid Ronald like a boat leak. For weeks, nobody would speak to him, visit him or offer assistance. The wives joked among themselves that from now on we were going to be nicer to our husbands.

Bill felt very badly that Ronald was being cut off from the rest of the cruising community and decided to pay him a visit. As we rowed toward his boat, we could see him sitting in the cockpit reading.

Bill called out, "Good afternoon, Ronald. How are things going?"

Barely looking up from his book Ronald replied, "Fine until some loud-mouthed American disturbed me."

Bill kept on rowing. We never saw Ronald after Margarita. I don't know what became of him.

Upon arriving at Margarita, our intentions were to stay long enough to provision and then hurry to the Panama Canal so we could cross the Pacific and spend the typhoon season there. But something happened to change our minds.

Mike and Liz on *Apolima* invited us over for dinner. We met for the first time earlier that day in the chandlery when Mike struck up a conversation with Bill. Canadians, Mike and Liz retired twenty years earlier and had been cruising ever since, sailing around the world twice and circling both South America and the Antarctic Peninsula with a dog and two cats on board. As genuine salts, they considered it an obligation to mentor us newcomers, warning about diseases in the Pacific, pirates in Indonesia and the hazard of fire on board. The warnings all stemmed from personal experience. Their previous boat caught on fire and sank and they traced the origin of the fire to a box of dry chlorine that spontaneously combusted because a bit of moisture got into the container. As they spoke, I was disturbed by the knowledge that months before, I placed the same type of dry chlorine on board *Alicia* to add to the water tanks. As soon as we got home that night, I told Bill what I had done and we removed the chlorine that night.

"What are your plans for the hurricane season?" Mike and Liz asked.

"We're going through the Panama Canal and spend the season in the Pacific," Bill said.

"Why are you in such a hurry?"

Bill explained that we wanted to sail around the world in three years and our schedule required us to be in Polynesia by June.

"Do you have to go back to work?"

"No," said Bill.

Mike leaned forward, looked Bill in the eyes and said, "Then slow down and enjoy it. You'll be glad you did."

When we returned to *Alicia* that evening, Bill took me in his arms. "Honey, do you like it here?" I didn't know what was on his mind. Smart man.

"Um, hum."

"I like it here, too," Bill continued, "When I planned the itinerary, I thought we'd skip South America. I had a vision of danger lurking around every corner but it's not like that at all. Don't you think it would be nice to relax for a while? We've been pushing pretty hard and sailing continuously for the last six months. We could both use a rest. What do you think?"

Stop sailing for a while? How could I argue with that?

We settled into a "normal" routine in Margarita. The villagers treated us like family and we responded equally. We began acting more like residents than tourists for the first time since setting sail. It didn't take long to reach the conclusion that if we were going to stay we needed to learn Spanish. Especially when I went to get my hair touched up to cover the gray and came home a bleached blonde. I knew I was in trouble when they placed me in the chair, put a tight plastic cap on my head and yanked my hair through the holes with a crochet hook. When the process was done, they raised me back into a sitting position. Not recognizing the person staring back at me in the mirror. "Ay, yi, yi." I muttered my first Spanish words. It was fun for a while. And what did I care. I would never see any of these people again. I'd just have fun while I could. But, blonde didn't look good on me. As soon as my Spanish was good enough, I returned to my dark locks.

Very early each morning the fishermen placed their nets in a circle around our anchored fleet. We watched and waited for them to retrieve their nets bulging with the weight of the captured fish. When the fishermen completed their daily routine, we hopped into our inflatable and rowed ashore. The breaking waves made it impossible to land the dinghy on the beach and stay dry, so we would end up with wet bottoms, fondly known in the cruising community as "dinghy butt."

After dragging the dinghy to a safe spot and locking it, we threw our backpacks on and would be on our way. We greeted the fishermen as they cleaned the morning catch and placed the filets on palm fronds for salting and drying. Passing the bocci court where the fishermen bowl and gamble every evening, through the little village with its thatched roof houses, we arrived at the main road and waited for the bus to take us to the town of Porlamar. By the time we got there, our bottoms were dry and we stopped to enjoy a cup of freshly squeezed orange juice from the vendor on the street corner.

After Spanish class, we would take a bus to the Hilton hotel to pass the rest of the day. While Bill played tennis with the professional, I sat by the pool with a good book. Later he joined me for lunch, a walk on the beach and we would end the day with meringue lessons. The relaxation was marvelous and I just sat around listening to my thighs grow.

Early on a Saturday morning, there was a knock on the hull. "Can Bill come out to play?" It was Jack, a retired airline pilot, from Spirit. Jack and Brenda had been cruising the Caribbean for three years.

"The last time we saw you, you were wandering around Marigot. That was four months ago. Come on aboard," said Bill.

"Thanks. What I really came over for was to ask if you would help me with a very important project. I've converted one of our water tanks into a rum tank and I need help installing a fountain. After all, with water more expensive than rum here, I had to take advantage of the opportunity."

It was true. The cost of living in Venezuela was a bargain. After the job was finished that evening, the total cost to entertain ten happy souls was less than $10.00 U.S.

Jim and Barbara on *San Silvestre* are a lovely young couple. Jim is a handsome Argentine. Barbara is a gorgeous, blonde Dutch gal. They live in Amsterdam and own a chain of restaurants called Argentine Steak House, working long hours for several months and then flying to their 48-foot yacht for a hiatus. Now we were together in Pampatar.

"How would you like to join us for a trip to the jungle to see Angel Falls?" they asked one evening. "We've arranged for a private guide to take us up the river in his canoe. We'll sleep in the jungle and then climb the mountain to view the falls. It should be interesting. Can you go?"

It didn't take long to make up our minds. Several weeks later, we left Margarita Island by air for Ciudad Bolivar on mainland Venezuela and caught a flight to the jungle town of Canaima.

Our introduction to South American wildlife came in the morning even before we started braving the interior. Several wild blue and red macaws smelled our breakfast of *arepas* cooking and decided to help themselves. The guides stood guard to keep our brazen feathered friends away from our plates, as otherwise we would be forced to make the jungle trek on empty stomachs.

We were fortunate to have Nosario as our guide. Nosario became a local folk hero when Frank Marshall directed the production of Stephen Spielberg's film "Arachnophobia" here. They hired Nosario for his knowledge of the jungle and navigating the rivers and cast him in a small part in the movie as a "humble Indian." His familiarity with the river was like poetry as he maneuvered around the rocks in the rapids with expert precision.

Thanks to the mild rapids, the six-hour canoe trip up the Carrao River to Auyan tepui (mountain) is a wet one. Toucans glide from tree to tree. Herons take flight over our heads as we intruded upon them in our thirty-five foot dugout. Iridescent royal blue flashes of light catch my eye. I have never seen anything like it and have to ask Nosario. He tells me they are morpho butterflies, found only in the jungles of the South American region. It was a thrill to get even a glimpse of them.

As we arrived at the campsite late in the day, there was still enough daylight left to explore and admire the environment, lush with ferns and bright blooming orchids. But darkness came quickly and the temperature dipped to 55 degrees.

A light drizzle began but that didn't stop Nosario from roasting the chicken on a long bamboo stick over an open fire. After dinner, as we chatted around the table in the dim light produced by a single candle, Jim felt something crawling up his leg. The unknown intruder vanished before we were able to find out what it was but it rapidly brought the social hour to a close with everyone deciding it was time to get to the safety of their hammocks.

The campsite became quiet and the last remnants of the candle continued to flicker. A mouse appeared and began to eat the cheese left on the table. Aware of his presence, I lay alone in my hammock, staring at the rafters above me. There was movement among the beams. "Look Bill," I said. "There are rats all over the ceiling."

"Go to sleep. I can't do anything about it." At some point, I must have fallen asleep for I awoke the next morning with the smell of coffee brewing.

After breakfast we began our climb to Angel Falls and Nosario warned us, "Be sure to watch out for the *venticuatro*." Almost one inch in size, this lethal ant gets its name "twenty-four" from the one-day fever it produces. Not only is it very painful but it also can cause death to those who are allergic.

The climb to the top was steep and slippery from the heavy summer rains. Sweat-streaked and covered with mud, we continued upward, grabbing hold of the large boulders for support. The density of the jungle shut out the sunshine but not the heat. Regardless, vibrant red flowers—so bright they resembled cheap plastic ones—were thriving. A harmless black snake slithered away into the undergrowth. Up, up until there in the opening we could see the famous world's highest falls, Salto Ángel, Angel Falls. A billowing mist cast rainbows of colors and created a delicious umbrella of cotton candy clouds in the sky.

On our canoe trip back to Canaima, we stopped along the river to meet Alexander Laime, a Lithuanian, who has lived alone in this jungle since the early fifties. The 80-year-old recluse lives in an area he cleared for a garden of bananas, papaya, pineapple, mangoes, and limes. His thatched-roof house is built out of the trees cut for the clearing. A plumb bob hangs by the entrance to indicate any damage from termites. Hundreds of books lined the shelves where he lived and he even built a separate hut he referred to as his "library" containing thousands more tomes.

Featured in *National Geographic*, Laime claims he saw three dinosaur-like creatures about three feet in length while searching for gold on Auyan-tepui in 1955. He proudly displayed his drawing of these reptiles that *National Geographic* said resembled plesiosaurs, marine reptiles extinct for 65 million years.

On the return flight, I took time to reflect on the memories we gathered at Margarita Island. It was time to say good-bye to the friends we made there. The sad part of cruising is saying good-bye so often. It's easy to think that we won't meet anyone quite as nice, but I have to remember we always do. I'm eager to see what comes next. Yes, the cruising life is finally getting hold of me.

We spent the summer in a marina in the mainland town of Puerto La Cruz, Venezuela, taking more Spanish lessons, doing more boat maintenance and generally passing the time with other cruisers also there for the hurricane season.

We were starting to meet more European cruisers, French, English, Swiss, and German.

And one Japanese couple. Neither one spoke a word of English when they began their trip on a thirty-two foot Japanese built cutter. They were anchored next to us and we watched them preparing to leave their boat.

The husband, Yoshio, was sitting in the cockpit indifferently watching his wife, Akemi, as she struggled to lift the cumbersome dinghy over the lifelines and into the water. Once she accomplished that difficult task, Akemi tied the dinghy to the boat and turned to lift the small, but heavy, outboard engine. Carefully balancing the motor on her shoulders she climbed down the boarding ladder, entered the unsteady dinghy and deftly placed the motor on the transom. When at last she got the motor cranked, a nod told Yoshio that she was ready for him. As though he was royalty, Yoshio stepped into the inflatable and arms folded, was taken to shore. I began to wonder if Bill might think he chose the wrong wife.

And then we met Anneke. I envied Anneke. Her husband, John, was sailing around the world and she didn't have to go with him. Instead she would fly to each port of call from their home in Mauritius. They would spend lovely times in exotic places and she would return to the creature comforts of her home while he would sail to the next destination. I liked that idea and entertained the possibility until I asked Anneke a question.

"Does he sail solo?"

"Never. He hires someone to help him. The new crewmember arrives tomorrow. When she gets here, I'll go home."

"She? Do you mean your husband is going to sail three months with another woman?" I asked.

"Certainly. I'm not worried. I've met her and she's ugly."

"Anneke," I said. "In two weeks, she won't be ugly to John."

Anneke stared at me and said, "You Americans are so prudish."

The more I thought about it, the happier I was to be with Bill full time. The desire to spend months at home without him didn't seem attractive to me. That was no longer an option I might have considered.

The tiny islands off Venezuela still don't attract the crowds like the upper Caribbean islands. Staying at several deserted islands, the only other life we encountered was bottle-nosed dolphins and our first whale. Seeing the whale, we kept a safe distance away. If an unwary boat comes between a mother and a calf, or a pair that has love on its mind, calamity often follows. Whales are known to attack a boat until it sinks. This one appeared to be alone and we stopped to watch him frolic.

At one island, Bill and I hadn't seen anyone else for days. Relaxing in the cockpit with a couple of good books, we looked up and saw a small dot on the horizon. As the dot grew larger, we surmised company was coming. But we never imagined our company would be a frail-looking elderly man in a tiny wooden dinghy.

Gradually, he drew closer. Finally, he arrived, inhaling deeply and letting it out slowly. His bare feet were clean and smooth from years of walking on some sandy island. His clothes were the typical cut off khaki pants and old T-shirt with some American logo both full of holes. Tired and worn-looking, the old fisherman held onto the side of *Alicia* and weakly pulled himself to his feet. Bringing two fingers up to his mouth he made the motion of taking a puff of a cigarette. "Fumada?" he asked.

"Oh, no. The poor old man wants cigarettes." It was the first and last time in my life I was sorry we didn't smoke.

Bill offered him water. He shook his head, no. We offered him Coca-Cola. He shook his head. We offered him crackers, cookies, anything—please accept something, Señor. He continued to shake his head. Looking disappointed, the old man turned and sat back down, picked up his oars and slowly rowed off into the horizon without saying another word. We have no idea where he came from or to where he returned.

We left soon afterward and made our way to Bonaire, the first stop in a small chain of Dutch islands off the coast of Venezuela, known as the ABC's. Aruba, Bonaire and Curaçao. Dutch, Spanish, English and Papiamento—a mixture of all three languages—are spoken here.

A diver's paradise, I named it "dive in-dive out" because we could scuba right off the boat and climb right back on board. Anchoring in twelve feet of water over a shelf, it drops off to eighty feet with some of the most spectacular diving in this hemisphere.

Catching up with Gordon and Joanie once again, we spent the days windsurfing and diving and organizing potluck suppers with the other cruisers.

At one of the group dinners, Bill and I met a lady who was alone and the three of us started chatting. She seemed somewhat melancholy but I merely presumed she was just one of the many wives who wasn't adjusting to cruising life. As she spoke, we couldn't believe what she was telling us. She lived through a nightmare no one should ever have to endure.

"My husband and I were on a passage headed for Bonaire. The halyard got stuck at the top of the mast and he needed to climb up to fix it. When he reached the top he hooked himself on so he could use both hands. He suffered a heart attack and died up there. I couldn't get him down. I was forced to sail the boat to Bonaire with my husband's body at the top of the mast for the next three days. When I got near Bonaire, I called on the radio and some cruisers came out to help me. I haven't recovered from the shock yet."

To lose one's husband like that is frightful. Among cruising couples, the greatest fear is losing your mate. The most common manner is falling overboard. It's no joke. It is almost sure death. Every safety precaution is taken to prevent such a dreadful thing from happening, but there is never a guarantee. Whenever we were underway, if Bill went forward to tend to the sails or set the spinnaker pole, I would always go through in my mind the steps I would take if somehow he fell overboard.

"First" I would tell myself, "throw the Man Overboard life jacket into the water. Next, run forward and lower the mainsail. Then run back, stabilize the boom and turn on the engine. Never take your eyes off him. Keep him in sight at all times while you turn the boat around." It's just impossible. So much to do in so little time.

In rough weather, the chances of rescue are slim with only one person left on board. It always made me worry when Bill left the cockpit without a safety harness, especially in rough weather. I worried for his safety—not mine. I could probably navigate to a safe harbor. But, if something happened to me, Bill wouldn't know how to open the refrigerator.

Fall came without the usual signs of red and gold leaves. There was no temperature change, only the usual warm trade winds blowing us west. Following these winds, we left Bonaire for Cartagena, Colombia.

During the passage, the skies were always cloudy, producing dark days and black, black nights. Even though we went through several gales, for the first time I wasn't seasick. Perhaps I was getting saltwater in my veins. On second thought, it had to be the Stugeron, a new seasick pill we found in Venezuela.

It was a tough call whether or not to stop in Cartagena. Stories flourished of the dangers there. Stories of cruisers being murdered as they slept while anchored in the bay. As we questioned in detail the tellers of the tales, we discovered that the deaths occurred eight years earlier. We decided to believe the few who told us it was safe now and not to miss this interesting city.

And so, after three nights and three days of rough-weather sailing, we arrived. Cartagena turned out to be a lovely 500 year-old city. The people are very proud of their history. Surrounded by forts and walls utilized for centuries to fight off the English, Spanish and Portuguese, modern-day Cartagena bustles with many new businesses in the ancient buildings.

There was the usual purse and necklace snatching during a fiesta, but this was not the scary, dangerous, gringo-killing city we imagined. More and more sailors are starting to make Cartagena a stopover.

Before leaving Colombian waters for the San Blas Islands, we made a stop in the Rosario Islands and visited an aquarium. There was the usual act of trained dolphins. A ho-hum act compared to the specialty performance of a group of trained nurse sharks. Yes, sharks. The crowd was kept spellbound by these predators of the sea as their trainer gave orders and the sharks obeyed.

He summoned them onto the platform so they were lined up side by side. With their tails still in the water and the upper part of their bodies out of the water, the trainer then called each one by name and gave instructions. One by one, the sharks shimmied backward off the stage and repositioned themselves again on the stage in the order the trainer instructed them. Then the trainer did something that no one else in the audience would have the nerve to do. He fed the sharks by hand. Little tidbits of fish they sucked right out of his fist. From that time on, whenever sighting a shark while diving, I would think of those trained sharks and wonder, how smart are they, really? Do they think humans taste better than mackerel?

We left Cartagena for the San Blas Islands, home of the Cuna Indians, a culturally fascinating people. The men have adapted to the casual dress and Spanish language of nearby Panama. However, Cuna women cling to the old customs and form of dress, still adorning themselves with thick gold rings through their noses and drawing one straight black line down their forehead to the tip of their nose.

The women are distinguished for their intricate reverse appliqué technique. Layers of fabric are stacked and shapes cut away to expose the layers beneath. The areas on top are then secured at the cut edges to those below with many invisible stitches creating a picture.

Many years ago, the women wore only skirts and decorated their upper bodies with tattoos. When the missionaries arrived here they made the women wear blouses or "molas." Improvising, the ladies then sewed their "tattoos" onto their molas. At first the artwork was simple, but over the years they incorporated pictures and it became very intricate and detailed.

The art part of the blouse is square, which forms the bodice of the blouse. Then puffy sleeves are added to the yoke and bottom of the blouse using polyester. Before polyester, they used flour bags. The mola is matching front and back, therefore only two molas are alike. Molas are sold both new and used, sometimes right off their bodies. Every Cuna girl is taught how to make a mola and part of her rite of becoming a woman is her first menses, her first haircut and her first mola. They celebrate with a two-day fiesta, complete with roast pig and firewater.

Molas have become big business in the San Blas Islands. Prices range from $5 for a tiny one to $100 for very intricate large ones. If a Cuna woman does not have any daughters, she will turn her youngest son into a girl—dressing him as a girl, complete with jewelry—and will teach him to sew molas to preserve the tradition and earn those ever-sought American dollar bills.

The Cunas have the highest rate of albinism in the world. Before the missionaries, they would kill these and any deformed baby. Now they believe the albinos to be a gift from God. Because their light eyes are so sensitive to the bright, tropic sun, albinos are kept inside making molas.

Punishment is severe among the Cunas. If one is found guilty of murder the penalty is to be buried alive with the body of the victim. Even so, there is some petty thievery aboard the sailboats. A yachtie reported the theft of some cassettes to a chief. The chief was visibly upset and the next day the cassettes were returned.

Cunas are quiet, polite and curious. They would row miles in their cayucas just to sell us molas, lobster, spider crab or conch. If we turned them down, they were noticeably disappointed but polite. They loved to row over just to look at us and talk. The women speak a little Spanish, just enough to sell their molas. They are very clever business people and will negotiate price but not to the point where their pride is hurt by selling their merchandise "too cheap."

Within minutes of our arrival in the San Blas, before even putting down the anchor, Edwino appeared. An enterprising Cuna, he presented us with a large crab. Still wriggling, the crab was placed in the sink for dinner later.

"My wife is making rolls. Would you like some when they are ready?"

Thinking it would be nice to meet his family, I asked if I could go with him to get the rolls. Climbing in the cayuca, I waved good-bye to Bill. After a twenty minute soaking-wet ride, we were still passing by little islands.

"Are we there yet, Edwino?" I kept asking as we passed each one.

"No, just a little further."

Finally arriving, I could indeed appreciate the effort they go through to come to our boats to sell their wares.

In a half-hour, Edwino showed me the entire island and introduced me to every resident. Sitting in his hut, my mouth watered with the aroma of the baking rolls. Made with coconut milk and prepared in a large covered kettle over an open fire, the hot rolls were presented by Edwino's shy wife.

Thanking her, I handed her two dollars. Gratefully receiving the money with a beautiful smile, she bowed slightly.

The return cayuca ride to *Alicia* was dry with the wind and waves at our backs. We gave Edwino gifts of sugar, flour, and water and thanking us, he returned to his family.

Hearing that the best quality molas were in Ciedras two hours away, I asked Bill to sail over there. Hundreds of men, women and children came out in their cayucas to welcome us. As we were preparing the dinghy, the chief arrived to explain why he didn't think it was a good idea that we come ashore.

"We are having a four-day fiesta. There is a funeral and we are going to have a baseball game. Many of our men are drunk. I don't want an incident. Please come back another time."

Disappointed, we thanked him and took his advice. Pulling up anchor, and returning to Holadesa Cay, we joined eight other boats. Together, we began plans for a Thanksgiving potluck party.

Bob and Sarah on *Small World* were new arrivals directly from Fort Lauderdale. Thanks to their large freezer, we enjoyed all the traditional food—turkey, sweet potatoes, pumpkin pie and apple pie—a treat after eating lobster and crab all week.

The time came to leave the San Blas Islands and make our way to Panama. Arriving in early December, we tied up at the Panama Canal Boat Club and Bill handled the paperwork and red tape of transiting the canal.

For months we heard stories of how dangerous it was to walk the streets of Colon, Balboa and parts of Panama City. From what I saw, it was all true. A ten-foot high chain link fence surrounded the yacht club. The manager wouldn't let us get into a taxi until he checked the credentials of the driver. The grocery store had four armed guards, two inside and two outside. As I chose items from the shelves, I was fully aware their fingers were on the triggers of long rifles. I could swear they were machine guns, but Bill says no. Every day, we heard a different story of a stabbing or robbery. Drug use was prevalent and evident on the streets.

Several American expatriates hung out at the yacht club bar. Colorful characters. Bearded, pony-tailed, and even one with an eye patch. The only thing missing was a hook in place of a hand. They told stories of seeking sunken treasure off the coast of Panama and of friends who disappeared, boat and all. One evening they invited us to their apartment and showed us beautiful solid gold Indian artifacts. Pieces of art in the form of lizards and frogs. Some weighed six ounces or more. They confessed that if the government knew they had these pieces they would be put in jail or worse. Under different circumstances, we may have been persuaded to purchase one.

When transiting the Panama Canal in a small yacht, it is required to have at least four people on board. Consequently, the couples going through the canal help one another handle the lines. From Colon on the Atlantic side to Balboa on the Pacific is a two-day trip. After completing the trip, the group leaves the boat in a yacht basin and takes a bus back to return the favor.

In the middle of the Canal is a small marina, the Pedro Miguel Boat Club, our home for the next three months. Instead of completing our transit, we stopped here for a layover, waiting to cross the Pacific until the first of April, the end of the typhoon season.

It's a lot like being at summer camp for adults. Each evening the wives gathered in the clubhouse and prepared dinner together. From the dining area we would sit and watch the huge tankers and luxurious cruise ships pass through Pedro Miguel lock. The canal is open twenty-four hours a day, seven days a week and there is a continual flow of boats going through, thus creating constant noise, turbulent water and lots of excitement.

As Bill and I made plans to fly back to Florida to see the family, I took time to reflect on the past eighteen months.

Adventurous things happened on this voyage, granted, but our first year of cruising was more a learning experience than an adventure. It was a period of adjustment. Not only did I have to learn how to sail but we were forced to conform to a whole new lifestyle in a fluid world. This new world of close quarters was surrounded by challenges. It was filled with a dichotomy of both total freedom and vulnerability. We had to develop new skills while adapting old ones to a new environment.

It is vital that a ship's equipment be functional at all times. The term "shipshape" has such a strong connotation because tidiness aboard ship is more important than just increasing one's comfort level—it's a safety requirement. Unlike houses on dry land, this home rocks and rolls and any object not secured during high seas can become a hazard at best, a missile at worst.

Yes, we reached a turning point. Our training period also taught us that the completion of our world cruise would be more comfortable on another boat. *Alicia* was a fine yacht, but built with speed in mind, not for living aboard. I was still having trouble sleeping in the V-berth and Bill sensed my discontent, especially when I announced I would prefer to sleep in the aft berth. Not picking up on my subtle message, he answered, "Okay, we'll sleep back there."

"What I'm trying to say is that neither bunk is big enough for the two of us. So I'll sleep alone back there." I'm sure Bill has a different account of this story, but no matter how you look at it, separate berths led to discussing changing boats.

Plans were made for a family reunion over the Christmas holidays with everyone meeting at Club Med in Florida. It seemed like the perfect place to entertain a group of eighteen, including children, grandchildren and our mothers. With none of the chores of everyday life, we could spend all our time enjoying one another. It was a happy time to be together after our long separation.

The week of family came to an end and Bill and I kept busy looking at boats for sale. We contacted our broker and friend David Walters in Fort Lauderdale. David's expertise in judging good yachts was invaluable to us in the past and we knew he would find a suitable yacht for us to circumnavigate.

David only showed us a few yachts before we found the right one. When we walked on board *Pegaso*, Bill noticed the rich varnished helm and the gleaming teak interior with its elaborate touches of white. He saw the large, immaculate, walk-in engine room and envisioned how easy it would be to maintain the engine and two generators. He examined the large forward workroom and noticed all the neatly stored tools he would need. But I noticed the queen-size bed and I knew this was the boat for me.

Bill decided to make an offer. After negotiating, we signed a contract with a clause that if it didn't pass the sea trial we could cancel. There was still a big doubt in our minds that just the two of us could handle a sixty-two foot sailboat. We were both thinking about the enormity of the task we were about to take on. Our fears were lessened somewhat by the knowledge that the former owners, Jorge and Herta Altamirano, sailed it around the world by themselves. And if they could do it, of course, we could do it. Couldn't we?

She is a sixty-two foot C&C ketch with a racing hull built to specifications as a cruising yacht in the custom yard. *Pegaso* means pegasus in Spanish. Deriving its name from the Greek word for "spring," it is said that pegasus was born at the springs of the ocean. Just like the winged horse in Greek mythology for which she was named, *Pegaso* sailed as easily across the water as its namesake glided across the heavens. We decided not to rename this one. There's a maritime superstition that if you change a boat's name, you also change her luck. Bill didn't want to take any chances or tempt fate. So *Pegaso* kept her name.

The sea trial off Fort Lauderdale was full of harbingers of good things to come as potential new owners of *Pegaso*. It was a bright and sunny day, the winds were fair, and the sea was calm. If that weren't enough, a dolphin followed in our wake as if nodding his approval.

Probably, what clinched it for me, though, is when I saw Herta jump up on the hard dodger and straddle the boom. Riding it like a cowgirl, she flaked the sail neatly while Jorge lowered the main. "Surely, I can do that," I thought, as I envisioned the two of us in a romantic South Pacific atoll.

The closing was held on Valentine's Day, 1992. They say the best two days in a boat owner's life are the day he buys and the day he sells. I only know we never regretted the decision to buy *Pegaso* and continue living Bill's dream of sailing around the world.

While we were busy with the boat survey, adding a few electronics, and hauling her to have the bottom painted, a crew was sailing *Alicia* back from Panama.

It was a sunny day when the crew arrived in Fort Lauderdale. With the boats tied together side by side, we took our personal belongings off the "old" and placed them on the "new." After two months of scurrying around getting *Pegaso* ready to leave, we began our circumnavigation for the second time.

To arrive in the Galapagos by early May and avoid the typhoon season, it was necessary to get through the Panama Canal as soon as possible. Since we had already cruised the Caribbean, we sailed directly to the Panama Canal with an overnight stop in the Bahamas.

After a day passage, we dropped the anchor in a lovely spot at a small deserted Bahamian island. We took the dinghy to shore to explore the island and snorkel the shallow reef. When we returned about an hour later, there were two rather sizeable men aboard *Pegaso*.

"No worries, friend. We were only looking for cigarettes. Don't get upset. We're leaving."

I thought they were very polite and didn't think too much about it until Bill explained that they could have been pirates.

"We were unarmed. They could have done anything with us and taken the boat. We were lucky." I noticed Bill avoided the words "torture and murder".

Seven years later, we would unintentionally drop anchor in that same spot and I would cause Bill a great deal of grief over that.

The night passage between Haiti and Cuba was crowded with boats. Abandoned boats floating upside down created a hazard and we had to keep a close watch in the area.

As soon as we arrived in Colon, Panama for the second time, we learned the people were planning a demonstration to protest the lack of interest the government showed them. To our advantage, rain caused the riots to be canceled and we were able to make haste out of Colon. Transiting the canal, we arrived in Balboa on the Pacific Ocean side the next afternoon. Friends in Colon told us by radio that five people were shot and killed in the city and the cruisers waiting to transit the canal could feel the effects of the tear gas and hear the gun shots.

Thus marks the end of the "trial" leg of our journey. Now, the adventure is about to begin.

7

Across the Pacific and Near Disaster

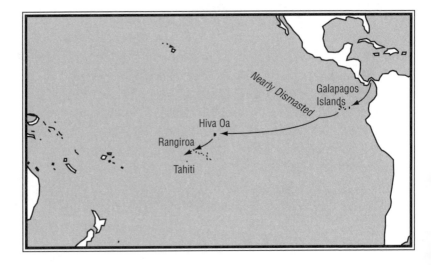

A sudden rush of water drove *Pegaso* sideways as the gates of the lock opened into the Pacific. Fighting to hold the boat steady, Bill steered hard to starboard and propelled us safely out of the Panama Canal. *Pegaso* had been here before but it was new to us. No more Atlantic chop. We were looking forward to the "peaceful" Pacific Ocean.

The southwest sail to the Galapagos Islands was uneventful. In my opinion, that meant it was perfect. With close winds of a comfortable fifteen to twenty knots we were on a beat and able to maintain a speed of seven and a half knots. (As you can see, I was learning a little about sailing by now). The waves were short and steep, not the big smooth rollers we hoped for. Nevertheless, *Pegaso* easily handled anything the sea wanted to give us and she remained even and stable. For me, that meant no seasickness. No seasickness meant no exhaustion and I was able to clean the boat and tidy up while underway, unheard of until now. The huge freezer was stocked with all our favorite foods and I enjoyed cooking in my big new galley. We both slept better in our new bed and so we were both in very good humor. Like magic I was transformed into a happy sailor.

We saw no other yachts except the bright lights of Korean fishing boats searching for squid at night. We knew they couldn't see us and so we were careful to keep well out of their way. There were reports that they would shoot at any boat that ventured too close. No matter who or why.

The good weather continued to hold and five days and 900 miles later we sailed into San Cristobal in the Galapagos Islands of Ecuador. As we entered the small bay, we could hear a high-pitched voice calling. It sounded like "Bill, Bill, Bill." Looking around, I expected to see a fellow cruiser standing on the deck of his sailboat waving his arms to get our attention. Finally realizing it was, in fact, the sea lions barking. Sea lions, completely unafraid of humans, make themselves at home on any boat left at anchor. These dry, volcanic islands are the only place on earth where the wildlife shows conspicuous indifference to humans. We would never experience another greeting like this one.

The tale is told that not too many years ago, any sailors stopping in the Galapagos on their way across the Pacific were welcome to explore all they desired. A few of these sailors took advantage of the animals' lack of fear and slaughtered great numbers, leaving behind carcasses and strewing garbage everywhere. Since then, a permit to cruise the Galapagos in a private boat is highly desirable but extremely difficult to get.

On an earlier side trip to Quito, Ecuador, it was arranged for us to obtain this special permit to cruise the islands on our own private yacht if we took a licensed Ecuadorian naturalist aboard. We read the papers written in Spanish, signed by the Secretary of the Navy and the Minister of Defense of Ecuador and it looked in order to us. As our Spanish was far from perfect, we showed them to Jorge and he was impressed.

"Absolutely," he said. "These papers are very impressive orders commanding them to allow you to explore any island you wish." With high hopes, we carried these papers for several months. Now, with papers in hand, we visited the port captain.

"We would like to make arrangements to hire a naturalist guide to take us to each island."

After carefully reading our papers the port captain wanted to know, "How did you get such important papers? Nobody can get permission to visit the islands in a private yacht."

Explaining we had friends in Quito who arranged the papers for us, he looked at us warily and said to come back tomorrow.

The next morning we were there bright and early. "I checked and these were indeed signed by the government officials. But you can't go."

"Why not?" we asked.

"It says here on page one that you may take a guide on your private yacht and visit all the islands." We nodded assuredly. "However, if you will notice, on page two it says you are only given permission to keep your yacht in the harbor for one week. During that week you may take any commercial guide boat and visit the islands. If such high officials didn't sign this, I could possibly be persuaded to let you explore the islands privately. I am sorry, but I cannot go against the authorities."

And so, with good intentions thwarted, we visited one island for one day on a very worn out guide boat. Departing early the next morning in an old 30-foot cabin cruiser, there was only time enough to visit nearby Española.

Each island retains its own characteristic flora and fauna. Blue-footed boobies, marine iguanas and sea lions predominated on Española Island. None of the animals showed any fear and we were able to walk directly up to the birds, focusing our camera lens just a few feet from them. The mockingbirds were especially brazen and would hop right across our feet if we didn't get out of their way. Keeping an eye where we walked to avoid stepping on an iguana was a good strategy. That is the charm of these fifteen islands named for the numerous land tortoises, *el galápago*, existing here.

It is a twenty-eight day average run from the Galapagos to the Marquesas Islands and the longest journey on the face of the earth between two points. Known as the "milk run" because of its reputation of being such a pleasant and easy trip, the 3,300-mile passage turned out to be anything but average for us. Without Bill's quick action, it could have been the end of our trip.

We were hearing news of a phenomenon that causes abnormal weather called "El Niño." From the moment we set sail on May 29, 1992, conditions did indeed become abnormal for this area at that time of year. Normal means winds ten to fifteen knots out of the east, seas calm and never above two to three feet. However, we experienced seas never less than 10 feet and winds averaging twenty knots and reaching forty knots for one twelve-hour period. These conditions aren't dangerous in a yacht our size and *Pegaso* handled the conditions remarkably well. We never felt in any danger. It's just that instead of an expected leisurely romantic excursion, we were on a roller coaster ride through the South Seas. Even as we wondered, "Where's the milk run?" we knew it could be a lot worse.

The trip began, as lengthy passages usually do, spending the first few days adjusting to watchman's hours. Passing the time reading or playing computer games, maybe even watching a movie on the video. *Pegaso*, with its two generators and large battery bank, never lacked power.

As usual, flying fish of all sizes and squid, probably attracted by the light, landed on the deck at night and died there. Hundreds of miles out of the Galapagos, we could still spot sea lions in the water. We think they may have been caught in the cold Humboldt Current that flows through there from Antarctica. A pod of whales was sighted not too far away. And of course, our favorites, the dolphins. On one occasion, there were dolphins as far as the eye could see. They loved to play in the wake of the bow and stay alongside for hours at a time, jumping and spinning. At night, they lit up the sea with streaks of light created by phosphorescence, our own private show.

It amazed me how far out we spotted sea birds, both large and small. A thousand miles from the nearest land and they never seem tired. Sometimes tiny land birds will get blown out to sea and find a boat and land there to rest, but they seldom live. The seagulls liked to fly close to our jib at night. The green light from the bow reflecting off the sail and onto their white bodies produced an ethereal exhibition, entertaining me for hours on my watch.

Each day we kept a scheduled rendezvous on the single-side band radio with a convoy of yachts headed for the same destination as we, Hiva Oa or Nuka Hiva in the Marquesas. Each morning began with a check-in, each yacht reporting their weather and position. The weather varied greatly within a fifty-mile radius and the night we went through the gales, no one else reported winds over twenty knots. Mostly, we were several days away from each other except for the night we passed John, Tom and Lisa on *Manipsha* and could see their masthead light. The radios were kept on during the day in case an emergency should arise. Voice of America provided some entertainment and news from home. In the evening, the convoy net reported again on weather and position.

On *Quest II* are Australians Bob, his wife, Toni, and friend Robert on their way home to complete five years around the world. Bob is a retired judge.

There's Lee on *Quest*. No, that's not an error. We met several boats with some kind of quest in the name. Lee is a single-hander. An American living in Haiti for the past ten years, his wife will make the passage via 747 when Lee arrives in New Zealand. A sick boobie bird joined Lee about 1,500 miles out to sea. Bill instantly named them "Lee and Boobie McGee." After force-feeding fresh fish to Boobie for a week, the bird died anyway.

Patsy and Chris, from England, are on *Jalingo*. Patsy, a gynecologist and Chris, an engineer, lived in Kenya many years. We would meet them off and on all the way around.

Ward LeHardy, a retired Army general, and Judy, his wife of thirty-five years, are on *Cormorant*, a 39-foot Corbin. We met them on the radio but would have to wait until we got to Rangiroa to meet them face-to-face. Most of those in the convoy were just voices on the radio until we joined one another in a future anchorage.

Four days and 700 miles out of the Galapagos, just as we were getting into the daily routine of the passage, something occurred that could have changed our destiny.

It was one o'clock in the morning. We were flying along at a comfortable seven knots of speed with twenty knots of wind behind. Full jib, full mainsail and full mizzen. I was sleeping soundly in the aft master stateroom and Bill was in the cockpit on watch when I was awakened by the sound of an explosion. The intensity of the noise forced me out of a deep slumber and I vaulted out of bed. By the time I reached the cockpit, Bill was standing there looking around.

"What was it?" I asked. My first thought was that we had gotten too close to a Korean fishing boat and they were shooting at us. My heart was racing as I held my breath.

"I don't know," Bill answered. We stood side by side looking aft trying to find out what could have caused such a loud blast.

"What's that in the water?" We saw it at the same time. As our eyes focused in the darkness, we were able to see a solid steel rod skipping along beside us. It was the stay that held the starboard side of the mizzenmast.

We were about to lose the mast. Bill yelled at me to run below and get all the ropes I could gather. Losing the mast could be hazardous at worst, troublesome at best. In our case, it meant we would lose all radio communications, the radar, the lifelines, and the dinghy. It would also leave a hole in the deck allowing water to get below. In the case of a storm, this could be a dangerous situation. We had to react immediately.

Bill ran to the mast and released the halyard holding up the sail. It was full of wind and Bill tugged hard to get it down. When he did this, the mast began to sway. Positioning himself behind the mast, Bill straddled the seat of the helm, wrapped his arms around the mast and held on. With the autopilot on, the boat was still making way and we were tossing about. There just was no time to do anything else but to get that mast stabilized. I grabbed the first rope I could find, handed it to him and ran below for more.

Bill was screaming directions. The look of fright on his face jarred me into realizing how serious this was. He never raised his voice before and I knew we must be in real trouble.

The taste of bile came up from my stomach and I forced myself not to panic. "Oh, God, please let me stay calm so I can help." My hands shaking, I passed a rope to Bill.

"That's not big enough. Get another one."

I reached around and grabbed a larger rope. He took it and tied it around the mast and passed the end to me. "Wrap it around the winch. Hurry."

I tried, but I wasn't fast enough. The mast was going, bent at the bottom from the strain and swaying with each movement of the boat. I wrapped the rope around a winch and using every ounce of strength I could gather cranked the rope as tightly as I was able.

"Another one. Get me another one." Bill was breathing heavily under the weight of the fifty-foot, three hundred-pound swaying column.

He swathed a second rope around the mast and I led it to another winch and pulled the rope taut. Bill continued to struggle as the boat made way and pitched in the sea.

"Get another." We struggled to get a third line around the mast. It was beginning to steady now.

"Another." Bill said. Exhausted by now from fighting to hold up the mast, his voice was losing volume. Line after line went around the mast, tightly back to a cleat and at last the mast was stable.

Hours later, weak from fatigue and too frightened to sleep, we lay in the cockpit and watched the sun rise. For days, we could both taste the bile still in our stomachs. Any tiny lurch of the boat, any little squeak caused us to flinch. It was months before I was able to relax.

The mast stayed solid until we reached Tahiti where the stay was replaced. What happened to us was unavoidable. Before leaving Fort Lauderdale, all of the rigging was carefully inspected. A tiny stress spot in the solid steel rod was undetectable because it was inside the mast. There was just no way to foresee what was going to happen.

There are two lasting impressions from living at sea. One is the sea itself. I learned to respect her, always recognizing that she was in control, offering us both her gentle bliss and her wrath. The best we could do was adapt to her moods, meet her challenges, and never lose respect for her dominating power. You can never conquer the sea. You can only conquer her moments, recognizing all the while that she is the teacher and we are the pupils. Living on the ocean is a never-ending learning experience. It has to be if you hope to survive. The lifestyle is constant. You grow accustomed to being surrounded by water and, as someone once observed, that's just the top of it. The dolphins and the birds become your friends, often being traveling companions and the only other living creatures you come into contact with for days and weeks on end. The sight of land is always an adrenaline rush and each port is both the same and different. We never lost the excitement of anticipation at meeting new people and being introduced to a strange, new culture. That, too, was constant. Change became the norm.

The other formidable impression is the divergence of personalities you encounter who share the lifestyle. Friendships formed through cruising the high seas create a bond unlike any others. The common experiences shared manifest an immediate connection between strangers that normally takes years to achieve under normal human conditions. Once again, it's the sea. Her dominance is powerful enough to influence relationships. If you are one of those within her grasp, you immediately recognize and bond with others who follow the same lifestyle.

Seventeen days after leaving the Galapagos we reached the Marquesa Islands. The sweet aroma of tropical flowers from the mountainous, green island welcomed us as we entered the bay of Hiva Oa.

Expecting a Hollywood scene of natives living in tiki huts and wearing grass skirts, Bill expected to be greeted by bare-breasted beauties bearing leis. Instead, we found ourselves in a modern French village with everyone driving four-wheel drive Toyotas and wearing T-shirts with cutoff shorts.

Convinced the mental picture we carried all these years was real, now we suspected we were victims of some tourist council's public relations strategy. Duped by an ad agency's best effort.

That didn't discourage us. We were able to find a lovely, quiet anchorage satisfying our longing for the lonely little hut nestled among the palm trees, looking out on a white, sandy beach.

Our Polynesian dream was rekindled when we arrived in Rangiroa in the Tuamotu chain. Flat, with palm trees and beautiful clear water, we finally found what we were looking for in the South Pacific.

The Tuamotus consist of eighty ring-like coral islands called atolls each enclosing a lagoon. The passes or inlets are treacherous to navigate and have to be timed just right to avoid the tide and shallow coral heads. Once inside the atoll, someone has to keep a close watch for the coral, usually by climbing the mast. On board *Pegaso*, that is a "blue" job. Bill climbed the main mast—the mizzen was still out of commission—and I took the helm. Calling down instructions, I would steer where he directed.

Anchoring off a small French resort with five other yachts, it was here we met a couple that would become very dear friends, Morgan and Jane Lucid on *Trinity*, a 48-foot aluminum Kantor. Morgan, a retired cosmetic surgeon, and Jane, a retired family counselor, left from California to begin their trip around the world. They enjoyed many of the same activities we did and were taking the same route.

Diving in Rangiroa is considered by some to be the best in the world and is famous for the abundant varieties of sharks inhabiting the outside rim. It is commonly believed these sharks are not interested in a human meal because of the copious amounts of other fish in the water. Assured by the dive masters that the sharks were not aggressive and that we would be safe, the four of us set our sites on diving Shark City.

The dive boat took us outside the lagoon into the open sea. Timing it perfectly for the tide to sweep us through the pass, we positioned ourselves and dropped into the water. Descending until we reached a comfortable position of sixty feet, it took a few moments to adjust to our surroundings before the current swept us away and through the pass. So strong was the current that we used our flippers for steering rather than propelling. Never in all my years of diving had I seen so many fish in one area. Just above our heads was a cloud of barracuda. And just below us we were about to descend into a throng of sharks.

In the dive group was Dominique Santorini, an illustrator for Jacques Cousteau. With a grease pencil and white board in hand, legs wrapped around a rock, he sketched what we were witnessing. Grey sharks, white-tipped reef sharks, black-tipped sharks, hammerheads and many more. Hundreds and hundreds of sharks.

We were so fascinated that we didn't have time to be frightened. At the end of the dive, someone reported seeing a fifteen-foot hammerhead gulp down a six-foot black tip. Thank goodness there was certainly plenty of other food to keep them satisfied.

It was here in Rangiroa that we at last met face-to-face with our friends from the radio, Ward and Judy LeHardy on *Cormorant*, one of the most remarkable couples we met along the way. Ward is a retired brigadier general. It is an interesting paradox that a career army soldier would become a sailor after retirement. Merely another indication of the wide diversity of backgrounds among people attracted to life at sea.

Many evenings, sharing tales in the cockpit, Ward entertained us telling "war stories." It was a welcome change from the typical conversations of engines, sails and weather to hear an insider's view of the Gulf War, Vietnam and the military in general, especially coming from one of the top brass in some of those campaigns.

Ward's father, a Naval officer during World War II, died when his ship, the USS San Francisco, engaged in close, direct combat with a Japanese battleship and sank in the Solomon Islands at two a.m. on November 13, 1942. Ward's mission was to be at that exact spot on the 50th anniversary of his father's death. What a tribute from son to father. Only a soldier would go to such lengths to pay homage to another soldier. Deeply moved at the display of honor shown by this warrior toward his father, Ward and Judy are indelibly fixed in our memory.

As a footnote Ward and Judy write: "Dear Alicia, Of course it's okay to tell our story in your book. And I think you know we got to that spot exactly fifty years later ... to the minute. Interestingly, once there, we definitely got the feeling that we were trespassing on sacred seas ... and that we didn't belong. But I needed that moment of 'closure' ... and got it."

8

Tahiti to New Zealand

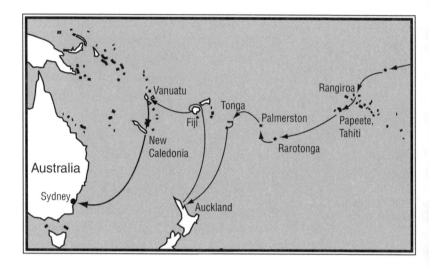

Most of 1992 was spent sailing the South Seas visiting the countless tiny islands that dotted our route to New Zealand.

If we knew how much we would enjoy this area, we would have planned to stay longer in the Tuamotus. The primitive, unspoiled islands were exactly what we were looking for. Brilliant blue clear lagoons. Flat, calm and comfortable anchorages snuggled safely behind reefs. The people, not influenced by tourism, had no use for money. The French government took care of their greater needs and their gardens cared for their alimentary needs. But anxious to repair the mast, we set sail for Tahiti.

After the pure and simple beauty of the other French Polynesian islands, Tahiti appeared fast-paced and worldly with its flurry and movement. Cruising yachts from all over the world heading west assemble here during July. It is the center for supplies and tending to repairs and maintenance. Replacement parts were waiting for us at the airport and Bill spent two days repairing the mizzenmast.

This was the first place in months where we could restock the freezers and enjoy plenty of fresh lettuce. Funny how this simple, common food that we have always taken for granted became a craving of sailors. You don't realize how much you miss it until you can't have it. It wasn't unusual to see cruisers greedily snatch the decorative green garnish on a beautiful plate skipping the meat or cheese at a buffet.

Convincing my mother and sister to come and cruise with us here wasn't difficult. Mom is a seasoned traveler and she was born ready to go anywhere. Carmen lives in Nebraska and as an avid sailor, she was eager to join us wherever we were.

She's an interesting person, my mom. Let me tell you about my favorite lady, my hero. Mom was a liberated woman before there was a name for it. But she was never confrontational about it. She never lost her femininity while she "did her thing." In her younger years, she was a champion springboard diver. But golf was always her favorite sport. She won the West Palm Beach Country Club Championship eight years in a row and they finally asked her to stop playing in the tournament to give someone else a chance.

She was never a housewife. As a matter of fact, she never did learn to cook. Never wanted to learn. We kids always said that we were the only ones in the school who thought the cafeteria food was fantastic. If we were naughty, she would send us to bed with dinner. One memorable Thanksgiving she invited a group of friends over for dinner. After they arrived, she took the turkey out of the freezer. Dad had to take all of us out to eat.

To get in eighteen holes of golf before work, Mom and Dad used to get up every morning before the sun came up just to be on the first tee at the crack of dawn. One fateful morning, Mom made a bet with a pilot playing in the foursome and won her first flying lesson. There was no holding her back from then on. She advanced to become a private corporate jet pilot with over eighteen thousand hours of flight time when she quit counting. She has taught or flown many famous people.

Dad was a golf professional. Both Mom and Dad worked sunrise to sunset, seven days a week for forty years. They never had a day off for any holiday. But for them, it wasn't really work. They loved what they were doing. You couldn't call us latchkey kids. It was safe in the Fifties. No one ever needed to lock their doors. We spent many hours at the beach with Mom and at the golf course with Dad. Yes, looking back on my childhood, it seems like one great big vacation.

Mom has a sweetness and naiveté that ingratiates her with anyone who meets her. She visited us often on our trip around the world. Any yachties who met her still remember and ask about my Mom. In her late sixties, Mom lost her right eye to cancer. That didn't stop her from flying, though. And she was one of the very few who could still pass the stringent FAA recertification and retain a pilot's license with one eye. Mom quit flying a few years ago when the cancer began to attack her one good eye. Like everything else in her life, she faces this one head on, bravely. It doesn't keep her from playing golf every day. And beating most men, and me too—with one eye.

Recently, I said to her, "You know, Mom, I just realized that to be considered as good a pilot as any man, you really had to be better than a man. Isn't that right?"

"Yes." She thought for a moment. "But it wasn't that hard." Thanks for everything, Mom.

As fate would have it, while performing the routine post-sail duties after anchoring at Huahine, Bill lost his footing and fell from the mast. We had just arrived from Moorea after doing an overnighter. Since it was a short trip yet busy with traffic, Bill shared watch all night and was tired.

When we neared land in the morning, Bill went forward, loosened the halyard and let the sail drop. It fell neatly between the lazy jack lines and onto the boom as it was supposed to do. Approaching the beach under power, we carefully chose a spot to drop anchor. I went forward and let go the anchor, being very cautious to stay out of the way of the chain as it sped out of the locker. After making sure that the anchor was holding, Bill and I began to tidy up.

We placed the sail cover on the boom and hooked it at the bottom. Next, Bill climbed a few steps up the mast to fasten the top of the cover. As he did so, a large motor vessel passed close to *Pegaso* and threw out a tremendous wake. *Pegaso* lurched from side to side and Bill started to fall. As though in slow motion, I saw Bill's hands slip from the mast and his feet move out from under him as he came tumbling down towards me. I held out my arms knowing it was a futile effort, but hoping to break his fall. Bill hit the pulpit on his back and tumbled to the deck unable to move.

Bill wouldn't let us take him to a doctor. There was severe pain in his chest and we knew the impact must have broken some ribs. Any movement caused him to wince. He was unable to laugh or cough, stand up or lie down without pain. His suffering lasted for about six weeks and gradually he became well again. In the meantime, it was a good thing my sister and mother were on board. They were able to help me while Bill relaxed and his ribs healed.

Although Bill was unable to participate in any recreation, it didn't prevent us girls from playing all we could. I mention this primarily because we left Bill behind to rest as we manned the dinghy to explore snorkeling possibilities in the lagoon. To this day Bill regrets not going with us. Two beautiful, topless Polynesian girls joined us in their pontoon canoe.

Bora Bora, Raitea, Huahine, Tahaa. Wonderful exotic islands. More diving, snorkeling and beach parties with other yachties. But all good things must come to an end. Wiping away a tear, we waved goodbye to Mother and Carmen, promising to see them again soon.

Gradually, I have come to realize that the places we enjoy most are not for where we are but whom we are with. This includes of course, other cruisers and visiting family, but also, the locals make a big difference. If we are able to communicate in their language or they in ours, it opens up a full panorama in our travels.

Three months after arriving in the Society Islands, we set sail for Raritonga in the Cook Islands. Piri Piruto elected himself our personal welcoming party in Raritonga. This fifty-two-year-old native is made of solid muscle. When Piri wasn't scaling a hundred foot tall coconut tree, he was demonstrating how to start a fire without matches. He treated us to a delicious meal of melt-in-your-mouth chicken, sweet potatoes, taro root, and coconuts and bananas wrapped in leaves all cooked in the ground. Piri had a special appreciation for the coconut trees. He explained why.

"I lived on a small island near here when I was a young boy," Piri began his story. "Every month a cargo ship would stop and deliver dry goods and canned food. One day it stopped coming. For four years, everyone on the island ate only coconuts and fish. Then one day, four years later, the ship arrived again. That is when we learned that there was a World War. I still love the coconut. The coconut saved our lives and I am living proof that coconuts are good for you."

When we mentioned to the vegetable vendors that our next stop was Palmerston, their eyes lit up. "Ooooh, will you take a few things to our relatives there?" Assuring them that we would be happy to do so, they met us at the sea wall with baskets full of food. Loaded down with oranges, cabbages, tomatoes, flour, rice and more, we waved good-bye to dozens of smiling ladies in their long muumuus and left for the atoll island of Palmerston.

An Englishman by the name of William Marsters settled Palmerston in the late 1800's. He married three Cook Island women and kept each wife on a different island. He fathered twenty-two children. After old William died, all the wives and children moved to the largest island in the atoll. Today all fifty-two inhabitants of Palmerston are named Marsters. There are also quite a few Bill Marsters there and it tends to get a little confusing. But then it could be easy. Just call any male Bill and chances are you are right.

We were told that the Palmerston islanders are the most cordial people in the South Pacific. It proved to be true. As we approached the island, two men in a skiff sped out to greet us and show us where it was safe to anchor. They pointed to a narrow shelf near the reef that drops off hundreds of feet. It was important to drop our anchor right on top of this shelf. This didn't leave much room for the boat to swing. If the wind happened to shift directions, any boat anchoring outside can be blown on to the rocks. That's why the direction of the wind needed to be closely watched while staying there. Going through the pass into the lagoon was out of the question unless it was a small boat. We couldn't risk going through—even in our inflatable dinghy—because it was narrow enough to cause a puncture. As a result of all this, the islanders help any yachties passing their way and we became the "official" guests of Bill Marsters, Jr. and "Dr." David Tom Marsters, which meant that they were responsible for our welfare and happiness as long as we were in Palmerston.

Bill and David Tom announced that we were coming to Sunday dinner. It was not an invitation. It was a command performance. Promptly at noon, they came to pick us up in their aluminum skiff. Grateful to be in their competent hands as they deftly navigated through the treacherous pass, we could see the old wreck of a Japanese fishing boat and many jagged edges of reef.

We arrived barefoot. No shoes are needed here because there are no roads, only clean white sand. It is pristine and flat with many coconut palms from a now dead enterprise of copra. Gasoline driven generators are heard all over the island. The generators are used to run their large freezers for storing the fish that is shipped to market in Rarotonga.

Just a short walk to dinner. Past the church built 150 years ago with lumber from a shipwreck. Past the cemetery. Past a few aluminum houses with palm frond roofs and we arrived at our hosts' home in the middle of the island. Quickly introduced to the family, we were immediately invited to sit down and join the group. Seated with a few other guests, including a visiting priest, we waited for the family to join us. No one did. Noticing that we were not starting, the priest informed us that the hosts don't eat until the guests are finished. There was a pecking order. First the guests ate, then the hosts, and finally whoever prepared the food—the women and children—ate last. The dishes were washed between sittings and used again. As we ate, the daughters stood around the table shooing flies away from the food.

We ate heartily so as not to offend our hosts. Even when we were full, we ate a little more to show that the meal was delicious. Later we learned that for one to eat less is the courteous way. What was left was served to the women and children and if nothing were left, then they would just have to wait until the next meal.

The most interesting item on the menu was what they called bosin bird. It was very dark meat, smaller than a chicken and very tasty, quite like duck, but tender. After asking them to describe the bird we were eating, I was convinced we were actually eating a baby boobie. Obviously, this was a delicacy. Their delight in serving us this rare meal showed on their faces.

The rest of the meal was typical island fare, taro and the obligatory fish. Then there was something neither of us could identify. I thought it tasted a lot like styrofoam with the consistency of year-old Jell-O. Bill thought it was delicious, but what does he know? After all, this opinion comes from a man who also likes my cooking.

The island "doctor" invited us to visit his clinic. Dr. David Tom had no formal medical training, but he did have a small room and medicine, much of which was outdated. Remembering Morgan and Jane were still in Rarotonga, we contacted them by radio and told them of the need for medicine and supplies. Morgan was able to get an ample amount at the hospital in Rarotonga and bring them to Palmerston.

David Tom showed us a scrapbook signed by everyone who stopped in Palmerston on a sailboat since 1936. We counted them. Only eighty-nine others were there in the last fifty-eight years.

"Look here," David Tom pointed to the page. "I knew *Pegaso* was here before."

There it was. Jorge and Herta signed the book in August of 1987 on their circumnavigation in *Pegaso*.

The next day Bill and David Tom were back again with orders for us to board their skiff for another feast in their homes. This time lobster was the main fare.

On the third day, feeling guilty that we were taking up too much of their time, we decided it was best to move on and allow the most hospitable people in the world to get about their daily routines. As we were raising the anchor, Bill and David Tom approached in their skiff.

"Please, don't go. You must stay and let us take you lobstering."

Thanking them again for all the kindness extended to us, we explained that we had to move on. It was sad to leave these wonderful people who opened their hearts and homes to us. To be treated like family by strangers brought about the feeling of leaving home. All this in only 48 hours.

Looking forward to joining other cruising friends in Tonga, we left Palmerston. Five days and more than 850 miles later, we arrived in Neiafu of the Vava'u group.

Tonga is an island nation monarchy and was never colonized. Because Tonga is still independent, there are no resort complexes. Anyone arriving with a dream of traditional Polynesia would be delighted. Even though never conquered by a foreign power, it was greatly influenced by English missionaries. English is the second language and everyone we met spoke it fluently. The people are very devout Christians and there are strict Sunday laws of no work and no play. The Tongan version of the hula does not allow hip movements, only slow movements of the feet and hands with the ladies dressed in modest muumuus.

Tonga is made up of four island groups, consisting of 170 small islands—less than 40 of which are inhabited. Cruising in the Vava'u group is perfect—simple, calm and easy because of the proximity of the tiny islands. The scuba diving is among the best in the world. That made it a good place to upgrade our scuba certifications to advanced open—water divers under the tutelage of Revonne and Alex Deitz aboard *Sealestial*.

If you are a spelunker, you will love Tonga with its numerous limestone caves. Mariner's Cave on Nuapapu is the most interesting and its secret underwater entrance kept it hidden for many years. According to one of our guidebooks, the history of Mariner's Cave tells of a tyrant chief who learned of a plot against him and commanded that the main conspirator and all his family be drowned. Another chief with amorous feelings for the traitor's beautiful daughter ushered her to a secret cave to prevent her impending death. Eventually his daily visits, bringing food and comfort, won her heart as well as her gratitude.

The young man needed to find a way to get the young lady from her hiding place to safety in Fiji. Organizing a secret voyage with a group of others in his clan, they left during the night. When asked why he would attempt such a trip without a Tongan wife, he replied that he would get one along the way. True to his word, he stopped the canoes, dived into the water and moments later appeared with the girl. Two years later after hearing about the tyrant's death, they returned from Fiji and lived happily ever after.

After reading such a romantic story, visiting Mariner's Cave was inevitable. Inviting five other cruising couples to join us on board *Pegaso*, we pulled up anchor to search for the entrance. Following the instructions written by a local, we motored around the island looking for the features that were supposed to guide us to the secret underwater entrance.

"It says here to find the tall palm tree on the cliff."

"What do they mean 'find a tall palm tree'? There are hundreds of palm trees and they are all tall."

"But there is supposed to be one that stands out among the others. Look over there. Is that it?"

"No. That can't be the palm tree. It's the same size as the others."

"It looks taller to me."

So it went. On and on. Trying to find one tall palm tree on an island full of tall palm trees.

"Let's get a little farther offshore and see if one of the trees looks a little taller than the others."

Backing off another two hundred yards, we continued to go up and down the coastline looking at the top of the cliffs for one lone tall palm tree. At last, we thought we found it.

If you looked hard enough and used your imagination, the tree did look a little taller than the others. Directly underneath the palm tree, on the side of the cliff, was the second distinct sign we were told to look for. A streak of white ran through the black rock, appearing as though someone tossed a bucket of paint on the side of the cliff. Below that should be the underwater entrance to the cave.

Now it was necessary to coordinate the logistics of this exploration. The cliff dropped right off into the water and there was no beach. Since there was no shore, there was nowhere to anchor. Someone had to stay aboard the boat at all times to maneuver around the area and everyone would have to approach the cave by dinghy.

Not knowing what to expect, the first one to attempt to enter the cave was by far the bravest. How far would we have to swim underwater? How deep is the entrance? How long do we have to hold our breath?

Taking turns in shifts, each one of us got a chance to try to enter the cave. Putting on flippers and masks, we slid into the water over the side of the inflatable and swam over to what we hoped was the entrance. The swelling tide pushed us toward the side of the cliff and then pulled us back in the opposite direction. Heads bobbing in the water, we looked at each other and wondered who would be first. Taking several deep breaths and finally holding the last one in my lungs, I plunged down about fifteen feet. Visibility was crystal clear and unlimited. I could see a narrow entrance to the cave. Kicking hard, I swam thirty feet straight ahead and through the opening, finally emerging inside to catch my first breath. Absorbing the surrounding beauty, we peered in amazement. The sun reflecting through the entrance created an azure blue atmosphere throughout a cathedral cavern. Boulders and crannies provided a pew-like appearance.

The surge of the water in and out of the cave caused a mystical fog that crept slowly toward and away from you permitting you to alternately see well and then not at all. The same surge played games with the eardrums creating a popping sensation. With our flashlights, we explored the walls and found scratches of writing reportedly put there by whalers many years ago.

The fun didn't end at the cave. Returning to the anchorage, we celebrated the day with a potluck feast and fell asleep with dreams of ancient mariners.

The morning radio net in Tonga was better than the "Today" show. Each day, Linda and Don on *Green Dolphin* entertained us with newsy little items such as who found the best bananas in the marketplace. Or where you could trade your Tupperware with the missing top for a half-used oil filter.

We just happened to have an extra short-wave radio that was taking up space and we asked the net if anyone needed it for an anchor. A voice came back and suggested we donate it to the school. Good idea, we agreed.

In Tonga, the schools are divided into different church groups. The Methodist school, the Mormon school and the Catholic school. Education is free and compulsory and the literacy rate is 100%. Western wear is popular. However, uniforms, such as for police and school, are still wrap-around skirts for the men.

The first school we approached was the Methodist school with a student body of about two hundred children from first grade to the twelfth grade. Visiting Mr. Garibaldi, the principal, we asked if they might have any use for an old world-band radio. Such a fuss was made about receiving the radio that he wanted us to present it to the school at a special assembly.

A date was set for the following Saturday and we were invited to be the guests of honor at a feast. Seated on the dais, Bill was asked to make a speech. After the presentation and much applause, the feast began.

Eating order was the same as in Palmerston. First the honored guests, next the men, finally the women and helpers. It didn't matter that there was a vacant seat at the table. No one ate out of order.

On each table was a roast suckling pig, taro, papaya, coconut, and their version of squash that looks like our pumpkin. After the meal, the children presented a program. Each class performed a dance and song or skit. During the performance, the parents and guests approached the performers and stuck paper money to their well-oiled arms and shoulders. The people were as generous with their paangas as they were with their food, with all the money going to the school.

Before leaving, we visited one of the most remarkable women we met while sailing, Mary McCollum, a 67-year-old retired schoolteacher from Eugene, Oregon. Mary sailed here single-handedly on her twenty-four-foot sloop *Mighty Mary II*. We met Mary in Tahiti and had seen her several times along the way. Mary believes she may be the oldest woman sailing the smallest yacht alone around the world. It's a good bet she's right.

On our way south we stopped in another group of the Tongan Islands, the Ha'apai Group, anchoring near a tiny island that appeared deserted. We turned on the radar to get an idea of the size of the island. It was only one mile long and one half-mile wide. With the binoculars, I could see a beautiful beach full of shells and didn't waste any time getting there.

Since this was obviously a deserted island, I donned my tiniest bathing suit and we went to shore. Pulling the inflatable up as far as possible to keep it from being carried out by the incoming tide, we began our walk on the beach. It was a shell lover's heaven. Each time I found another shell, it felt as good as going on a shopping spree on Worth Avenue in Palm Beach. There were perfect specimens of nautilus and tuns, very fragile and hard to find in such good condition. Comfortable that we were the only ones to discover this little paradise, I became lost in the thrill of the hunt when Bill noticed a sign. Climbing the dune to get a better look at the handwritten sign, we gulped when we read: Warning. Danger. This is a prison island. No visitors allowed.

Looking around, I could have sworn there were a thousand eyes watching us from the bushes. My peaceful shell expedition turned into a paranoid outing. Bill grabbed me by the hand and we dashed back to the dinghy. It seemed to take forever before we were back on *Pegaso*. It was too late in the day to go to another anchorage. Forced to spend the night there, neither of us slept very well with visions of prisoners swimming to the boat and taking us hostage.

Leaving Tonga, we sailed South to Auckland, New Zealand. The winds couldn't have been more cooperative. It was a superb sail and an amazingly fast time of five days and nineteen hours. Little did we suspect that six months later along the same path, we would have the roughest ride of our entire trip.

9

New Zealand

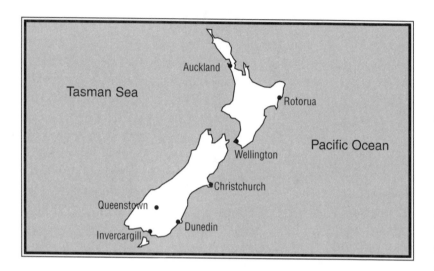

The most common question we are asked is, "Of all the places you visited, what was your favorite?" Always our answer is that New Zealand is our favorite "developed" country.

Situated below the equator, in only 100,000 square miles of land, New Zealand has all the beauty, all the natural resources, and all the recreational activities that any country could offer. Comprised of two large islands, the North Island is generally temperate with the cold climate occurring in the South Island.

Surrounding ocean waters support abundant sea life and recreation, from whale watching to scuba diving, from sport fishing to gathering fresh mussels, swimming with dolphins, skiing or rafting. This tiny country boasts plains and mountains, volcanoes and glaciers, hot springs, geysers and fjords. It is rich with mineral deposits, timber and many indigenous plants not found anywhere else in the world.

The healthy lifestyle of the people is probably due to the lack of choice on the television. Two stations serve the entire country. Maybe that is the reason parks are full of families playing soccer, rugby, tennis or skiing, rafting and tramping (hiking). And of course, as we know, they are avid sailors.

As soon as we sailed into Auckland and tied up at the marina, there was a knock on the side of *Pegaso*. "Is Jorge here?" The voice wanted to know.

We went above and introduced ourselves to Graham Jordan. "No, we bought *Pegaso* from Jorge and Herta nine months ago."

"Good on ya, Mate. She's a fine yacht. My wife and I will be by to pick you up and bring you to our house for dinner tonight. See you at seven." With that introduction to the Kiwi hospitality, we were certain we would enjoy our six-month stay in New Zealand.

Auckland Marina overflowed with cruising yachts waiting out the typhoon season. During the birthday celebration for Jay on *Skywave*, we met a young woman whose courage touched my heart. Her leg was scarred and mangled and she walked with a distinct limp. Andrea, at age twenty-two, was a Kiwi champion swimmer. Six months before, she survived a shark attack while on a vacation with her family in Vanuatu. When I asked her about the incident, she was surprisingly eager to talk about what happened. Andrea explained that her reason for being so open about her misfortune was that she wanted to warn others how to prevent shark attacks.

"That's news to me," I replied. "I didn't know you could prevent shark attacks."

"Oh, yes, you can. And I wish I knew before I went swimming. I should have asked the locals if it was safe to swim in the bay where we were anchored. They would have told us that it was full of predatory sharks. There are certain areas that are safe and certain areas that are not. Sharks are also attracted to boats in an anchorage because of the scraps thrown overboard. Even if you are careful not to throw food overboard, they are attracted by the human waste that is pumped out."

And so, unaware of what danger beheld her, Andrea went for a leisurely swim by herself off the anchored yacht. She never saw the shark before it struck. Like a flash of lightening it clamped down on her lower right leg akin to a bear trap. Shaking its head vigorously and pulling backwards with all its might like a dog fighting for a bone, the shark pulled Andrea under. Willing herself not to panic or try to pull away, she balled up her fist and hit the shark in the snout. Her reaction saved her life. The shark miraculously retreated, leaving a gaping and jagged wound with the muscle ripped away in a single bite. Swimming back to the boat, she wondered when the shark would strike again. Certain this would be the end. Once on board, the most important procedure was to apply pressure and stop the bleeding. Her life was saved because someone on board knew the correct pressure point.

She found out later that others were not so fortunate. "I was lucky and lived," she observed, "but five others before me in that same area did not." Andrea was flown back to New Zealand and spent two months in the hospital.

As we trekked through the South Pacific, we grew quite used to seeing sharks while diving. Some areas were considered safe to swim with the sharks and in other areas the sharks had a reputation for being man-eaters. But after hearing Andrea tell of her ordeal, it renewed in us an apprehension of encountering any sharks.

Several of our unmarried children and my mother visited us here. Because they didn't all come at once, it gave Bill and me the opportunity to tour both islands several times. Our son, Todd, on December break from Ohio State, joined us on our first tour. Since his visit was going to be brief, we packed up the car and headed for South Island.

If you really want to know a country, get to know its people. The best way to know its people is to stay in a bed and breakfast. There are many B & B homes in New Zealand from which to choose.

A sheep ranch in Blenheim was our first stopover. Our hosts, Jean and John Leslie, raised 2,700 merino sheep on 1,500 acres of dark green grass-covered hills. Very early in the morning, we were awakened with the smell of bread baking. After a breakfast of mouth-watering hot bread, homemade blueberry jam, sausage, cheese and eggs, we joined John to round up the sheep and move them to a different pasture. The border collies were boisterous and eager to go as we opened the doors to their cages. Leaping out, they took off after the sheep. As John whistled through his teeth, each dog obeyed and moved the sheep left or right, understanding each nuance and tone.

This was an especially bad year on the ranch. They suffered their worst season of fly-strike fever, a disease caused when flies lay eggs in the wet fur of the sheep. If there is too much rain and the fur can't dry, the larvae have a chance to work their way down to the flesh and slowly devour the animal alive. We found several dead sheep and one just barely alive. John attempted to rescue the surviving sheep but was unsuccessful.

Just like her ancestors, Jean cooked in a wood oven. This same oven was also used to heat the house and water. In the evening she would spin yarn and prepare dough for fresh baked bread for the next morning's breakfast. It was as though we were somehow transplanted into a different period of time.

Because it was summer in New Zealand, all of our favorite fruits were in season—grapes, raspberries, peaches, nectarines, and naturally, kiwi fruit. Lunch was a pick-it-yourself feast of cherries—sweet, large and crunchy, the best we've ever tasted. Since produce doesn't have far to go to market, it is never picked until it has fully ripened, and the flavor is unsurpassed.

Traveling further south, we left the main highway for the backwoods and became cowboys for a few days at the B&B of Cheryl Dean and her husband, Jack. After horseback riding in the wilderness all day, nighttime was spent tucked away in an isolated hut conspicuously positioned in a picturesque country field. Breakfast was cereal and fresh—squeezed goat milk, left on our doorstep and kept cool by the crisp morning air. We did, however, have all the modern conveniences including a "long drop," Kiwi for outhouse.

Before she was married, Cheryl spent two years riding alone in the South Island, living under the stars. Now Cheryl and Jack live in a cabin made from the trees they cleared off the land. Her husband creates medieval musical instruments and they entertained us with a concert at the end of our two-day ride.

New Zealand became our playground. There is so much to enjoy. It seems somehow the entire island country is one gigantic theme park. I never would have imagined in my wildest dreams that we would attempt some of the things we did.

Bill and Todd started it. The two of them actually dived from a one hundred forty foot high bridge. Bungy jumping. Who would believe it? Two grown men, with nothing but a rubber band attached to their ankles, intentionally leaping into what looked like certain death. It was a horrifying sight to watch two men I loved plunge toward the bottom of the river below. Just before striking the surface of the water, a sudden flying jerk stretched the bungy rope and catapulted them back up. Bouncing up and down, back and forth, until it was finally over and a recovery team released them. Instead of nursing a number of expected injuries, aches and pains, there were two grinning guys complete with certificates and T-shirts boasting of their achievement. That started our wave of thrill seeking.

A day of white-water rafting in the Shotover River provided more excitement. Dodging rocks and ledges, the three of us spent hours swishing down the river with the current. At the last few yards of the trip, we maneuvered through a tunnel and over a small drop into the safety of the riverbank.

"Let's take a little rest from all this excitement and do something easy-like go for a little walk." I forget who suggested it—I'm sure it wasn't energetic Todd—but that's what we did.

The Milford Track has been called the finest walk in the world. Not only can one take pleasure from the beauty of the landscape, it is also historically interesting. At one time it was the main route across the tip of the South Island. The first European crossed the track in 1888 but the native Maoris used it before then. The thirty-four mile walk can take up to five days with a guide. Or you can hurry and make it across in three days. There are sleeping huts set up along the way. Fly-fishing will usually yield enough fattened trout for all. We chose to make a one-day trip going just far enough to have lunch and walk back to the beginning of the trail ready for less hiking and more thrills.

And more thrills are what we got. Like parachuting.

"What am I doing?" I asked myself. "I should be grocery shopping like a normal woman."

I was preparing to jump out of an airplane three thousand feet above the ground. The fear hit me the most during ground school—the formal training course provided to teach us what to do if Murphy's Law takes effect. We spent most of our time practicing what to do in case one of the hundred things that can go wrong during a jump does go wrong.

When the plane finally reached jump altitude and Bill and Todd leaped into the heavens before me, my fear disappeared . . . or maybe I was just too petrified to know that I was afraid. The instructor told me he had to kick me out the door. Whatever. I did it. And together, the three of us experienced the exhilaration of our first solo jump. Todd was great. He even landed like a pro—standing up. I did a drop and roll. Actually it could best be described as stumble and fall. But, we all agreed that it was something we wanted to do again.

That would have to be another time though. It was time for Todd to return to his studies and for the next set of visitors to arrive.

It's interesting how being in some exotic location will assure a visit from family. The only problem is, grown children are much harder to entertain than little ones.   I considered it my motherly duty to design a program equally as exciting for the others.

The day after Mom and daughter, Shari, came to visit, we headed to Parakai to do some tandem skydiving. Shari and I jumped. Mother co-piloted the plane. The Kiwis called us the "three generations of wild women."

Tandem jumping takes no skill because strapped to your back is an experienced jumper. Our coaches boasted as many as two thousand jumps assuring me it would be a stress-free event. Shari and I jumped within seconds of each other. As soon as our chutes opened, the coaches maneuvered us close together and we marveled at the wondrous experience of our rendezvous in the clouds.

Next, Shari and I shared the "Lost World" experience, an adventure involving a three hundred foot abseil descent down a narrow limestone shaft. This adventure began with a hike across a field to a small clump of trees. I wonder about the first person to discover this hole in the ground. It appears unexpectedly in the middle of the hammock and one step too many would send you tumbling into oblivion. After being outfitted with lighted helmets, straps and a few instructions, we sat on a fragile tree limb over the shaft while Steve, our guide, shackled us into our safety gear, the only thing between us and a sheer drop to the bottom.

Slowly, we lowered ourselves to the bottom. Once there we stepped around the remains and dried bones of livestock fallen from above, and continued our amazing expedition through the Mangapu Cave system. Mist filled the abyss as we carefully climbed over large boulders, traversed ledges and treaded across small streams of icy water. For hours, we worked our way through the maze until we came to a solid wall of rock and could go no further. A thin sliver of light shone one hundred feet above our heads. Steve informed us that the small opening way up there was our way out. He would ascend the ladder rope and promised to send a hoist down to help us up. Hand over hand, Steve ascended the rope and disappeared. Alone in the dark with Shari, I prayed he would make it to the top. Moments later the hoist came floating down.

As a firm believer in age before beauty, I didn't hesitate in volunteering to go first. It felt like it took forever to ascend, but after struggling for what was probably less than five minutes, I was breathing fresh air and welcoming the sun again. Shari followed soon after and never complained about being left alone in a dark, dank cave.

From there, we drove to Rotorua and did the "Awesome Threesome," beginning with a helicopter ride to the Rangitikei River. Our pilot swooped and dipped over and around the hilly scenery. Stopping to hover above a waterfall, he announced, "And that's the waterfall that you'll be going over on your rafting trip."

Shari and I both laughed at the joke—only to realize that he was serious. We really were going over that twenty-two foot drop.

When we arrived at the rafting grounds, we donned our wetsuits and crash helmets and proceeded to the riverbank for basic instruction. We were taught how to paddle, steer, and get down on command. Special attention was paid when he explained what to do when we were going over the decline. It was then I thought that I should have asked this question before signing up.

"Uh, excuse me," I said, "Could you please tell me what grade river this is? His answer sent chills up my spine.

"This is a grade 5."

Low-grade rivers (3 and below) introduce you to rafting, letting you employ basic rafting techniques and at the same time, give you a few thrills. Advanced rafters head for grade 4 and 5 rivers. It was a dreary day. Persistent rain kept the sun from shining. I was shivering and nauseous and I couldn't tell if it was the biting cold or nerves. Looking intently at Shari for any sign of fear, I was hoping that she would be the first one to quit.

"C'mon, Shari," I thought as the guide described the ten things to do in case you were caught in a whirlpool underwater. "C'mon, Shari, all I need is one chicken-out word from you and I quit."

I stared at Shari, hoping for an out, but all I got was a non-committal return stare. "Okay," I thought, "I've really got to go through with this."

Like the proverbial calm before a storm, the trip started out slowly, quietly stretching through incredible breathtaking scenery. But we weren't lulled into thinking this would be easy. Several exciting rapids followed as the river wound through the wilderness. After one short rapid fall, our guides maneuvered us to the side and told us that the big one was next. Apprehension set in, but it was too late to turn back.

"We have an 80% chance of flipping," our guide said. "Never let go of the rope. You'll come up under the raft if you don't let go. There will be an air pocket. Wait for us to flip the raft over and then climb back in."

Poised at the top of the fearsome rapid, we could see the wild churning of the water. Holding our breaths, we paddled over the precipice. The raft tumbled end over end and spilled all its riders into the icy-cold water below. I clung with all my strength.

I popped up gulping air and, sure enough, I was underneath the raft in an air pocket. Seconds later, Shari's head popped up next to mine. Her eyes were as big as saucers and we were both gasping from the shock of the 55-degree water. It was icy, it was frightening, it was traumatic, it was fun. Soaking wet, feet like blocks of ice, I wondered why I did this wild, heart-stopping, crazy thing. Soon, but not soon enough, our guides flipped our raft upright and we all climbed safely back in.

When it was over and I thought back about all the anxiety, I knew it was worth it. What a thrill. It's like some philosopher once observed "we all die, but not all of us live." This was living.

Returning to Auckland, Shari and I went riding on the beach. After three death defying acts—parachuting, abseiling and white-water rafting, what could be easier than riding? Right? Wrong.

In a full gallop, the girth on Shari's saddle broke and sent her flying through the air. She fractured several ribs and endured a lot of pain for the rest of her stay.

"After all that excitement and activity," Shari aptly proclaimed, "I never broke a fingernail ... only my ribs."

Now I was going to find out that all was not perfect in this paradise land. We were going to learn that medical care in New Zealand isn't the same as to what we are accustomed.

When Bill and I first arrived in NZ, we hadn't had the regular medical check ups that doctors back home recommended. It had been three years since my last exam so I called a gynecologist and asked for an appointment.

"What is your problem?"

"I don't have any problem. All I want is a pap test."

"Who referred you?"

"No one. I picked your name from the yellow pages."

"You have to be referred to a specialist by a general practitioner. Go see a g.p. and tell him what you need."

Bill and I made an appointment to see a doctor the next day. His office was one tiny room in an Auckland office building. He insisted on seeing us both at the same time.

"What's your problem?"

"Nothing," Bill said. "We just want an examination and my wife would like to have a pap test."

"Well, you look healthy to me. Why do you want an examination?"

"Because we wanted to make sure that everything is fine."

"If you feel well, then you are well. You don't need me."

That was our introduction to national medicine in New Zealand. Now we were about to have a similar experience with Shari's broken ribs. The week before, another rider had fallen and broke his ribs. They were still talking about how the doctor hadn't discovered a punctured lung and the rider almost died.

I put Shari in the car and we drove to the nearest clinic. The doctor examined her, diagnosed her broken ribs and said she could go home.

"I would feel much better if you would x-ray her," I said.

"Why?" he said.

"To see if one of the ribs has punctured a lung, or something."

"It's not necessary. She's fine."

"We know we're not citizens and I don't mind paying for it. Here's my credit card. Please x-ray her."

"It's not necessary. I have examined her thoroughly and she is fine."

"I don't care what it costs. Please just do it to make me feel better."

"You don't listen do you? I said she is fine."

"She has to fly back to the United States tomorrow, and for my own peace of mind, please."

"Madame, I said she is fine." He turned on his heels and strode off.

I felt powerless. It didn't matter to him that I was willing to pay for the care we wanted. What if something was really wrong? Because of the national health system and perhaps because there is no legal responsibility, a doctor will take fewer safety measures to prevent misdiagnosis.

Thank goodness he was right and Shari was fine. The two weeks my mother and daughter spent with us went by so quickly that it seemed to last only a matter of hours. But it was more than a visit. It was truly an adventure.

Ironically, despite all the risks Bill and I took during our thrill-seeking ventures, we suffered no injuries from our death-defying exploits. That misfortune occurred where it happens to most people . . . on the highway.

Knowing we needed land transportation during our six-month stay, we calculated that it was less expensive to purchase a car than to rent one. That's what most cruisers do. But the hard part is getting used to driving on the opposite side of the road. It's a common mistake for right-sided drivers to have accidents in left-driving New Zealand. That was our hapless blunder.

After putting more than three thousand miles on the odometer, we still made the dangerous mistake of looking the wrong way before entering a highway. We never saw the other car coming. He hit us broadside going full speed just in front of the passenger door. Another foot and we could have been killed in our flimsy Subaru. Both cars were a total loss, but thankfully no one was severely injured. Bill cracked a few ribs again. I received a cracked sternum from the seatbelt and bruised knees from the dashboard. Those in the other car had only minor injuries too.

You might wonder what happens in New Zealand in case of a bad accident. There are neither huge lawsuits nor huge awards. Compensation to injured parties is only for the amount of damages. Since it was our fault, our insurance company replaced both autos. The state paid for the minor injuries of the gracious gentleman who hit us. He was retired so he didn't lose workdays. It would be no use for anyone to complain of whiplash or headaches and that was the end of it.

After being landlocked for nearly six months, the time came to set sail for Fiji. There were lots of good-bye dinners and farewell parties with Kiwi friends and cruising friends, where we exchanged itineraries, hugs and kisses. But soon they were tossing us our lines and we returned to face what the briny deep of the Pacific Ocean had in store for us again.

10
Fiji

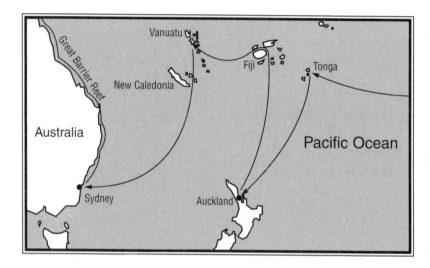

The second most common question asked us is, "Did you get in any bad storms?" I would answer " We were in a lot of very uncomfortable weather and I was afraid many times, but our lives were never in danger." This trip was to be one of "those" times.

Even though some consider it bad luck to leave on a Friday, we set sail anyhow for Suva, Fiji. We didn't really expect anything to go wrong because of a silly superstition and it didn't. But during this passage we were again reminded of the extraordinary power of the sea.

It took almost seven days to complete this northbound trip of 1,160 miles. Winds maintained a steady twenty-five knots with gusts to forty-five. Intermittent gales and storms hit us, but each time the sun broke through, it brought welcome relief from the cold we endured all through our New Zealand stay.

The seas were ten to twenty-five feet high. Rogue waves exploded over the decks, swooping seawater into the cockpit. On my night watch, a wave brought a flying fish with it and left it in the cockpit. It was dark and I couldn't find it among all the sheets (ropes) but its foul odor left no doubt as to its condition. Once the sun rose, the fish, victimized by the turbulent seas, was discovered and sent back where it belonged.

After being away from a boat's motion for so long, we were trying to regain our sea legs. It's amazing how quickly you forget the sensation of the world moving under your feet. Part of maintaining one's balance on a sailboat requires tensing the body. We almost felt like spaghetti the first few days, forgetting to brace ourselves in position. Getting bounced around, we endured a progression of minor cuts and scratches that Bill calls "boat bites."

I was especially pleased that the violent seasickness I once suffered was now a thing of the past. Facing a slight queasiness during the first few hours of the passage was insignificant compared to the extreme discomfort of what I endured before. I gave the credit to *Pegaso*. With her heavy keel and big round bottom, she sailed with a nice smooth motion. Whatever it was, I was glad that for me *mal de mer* was history.

Many of our fellow cruisers would fight the same battle and we debated what causes it. Could it be tension and fear, or just a propensity towards seasickness? Home remedies like ginger or pressure bracelets didn't seem to help. Bonine and Dramamine were useless. The transdermscope patches were downright dangerous. Our best discovery was Stugeron. This non-prescription tablet, if taken in the correct dosage did not cause any bad side effects. The only problem is that it cannot be bought in the United States and cruisers had to stock up in South America or Europe.

During our crossing, we kept in close contact by radio with the cruisers' radio net. All cruisers sea bound in the area reported the same conditions and similar experiences. Most suffered only minor problems, but two others weren't so lucky.

Muddy Water, a Kiwi boat, interrupted the net one morning to report that a wave hit his bow so hard that the bulkhead was cracked and he was taking on water.

"We may have to abandon," he told us. He was lucky, though, and was able to do a quick temporary fix and continue on.

Sea Music, with five Kiwis aboard, was not so lucky. They decided to drop their sails in the middle of a gale and drift. It was night and the exhausted crew went to sleep. They drifted onto well-charted Minerva Reef, nothing but a tiny, uninhabited atoll in the middle of the Pacific. The boat was a total loss, but luckily for them, Minerva is a favorite stop-off and three boats there saved their lives and personal belongings.

The tropics felt good after the cold summer of New Zealand. Entering Fijian waters meant that now we must keep close watch for submerged reefs. Even the visible reefs can cause havoc. The evidence is the rotting wrecks that dot the entrance to the big island. Snuggling into Suva harbor full of other cruisers from all over the world, we settled back to discover Fiji, our favorite "undeveloped" country.

Fiji consists of two large islands and more than three hundred small islands. Situated on Viti Levu, the largest island, is Suva, the capital, a large, cosmopolitan city. Bustling with activity, it boasts fifteen embassies and the University of the South Pacific. The British influence is still there, having left behind its colonial buildings and language. Situated on a hilly peninsula with mountains to the north and west, it catches the southeast trades, bringing rain nearly every day. In spite of the abundance of cloudy, wet weather, it's a fun place to stay with many excellent, inexpensive restaurants and movie theaters.

The population is 48% Fijian and 48% Indian. The rest are Anglo. Even though some Indians are third and fourth generation, they are still treated like strangers or guests. Indians are not allowed to own land, even though they are the merchants.

The Fijians are very uncomplicated people. Very straightforward, sincere and generous. They are a patriarchal society of very devout Christians. It was hard to out-give a Fijian and they preferred to be the last to give so they wouldn't owe us anything.

Circumnavigating Viti Levu, we stopped at several of the out-islands. Each time we dropped anchor, it was mandatory for the captain to give an offering of dried waka root to the chief to ask permission to stay. With the waka, they would make a drink called kava. The ceremony is taken very seriously and marks births, marriages, deaths and official visits.

Kava is a tranquilizing, non-alcoholic drink that numbs the tongue and lips. It is prepared by pounding the root in a hollowed log stump and mixing the pulp with water by hand in a large shallow wooden bowl. The water is then strained from the pulp through a cloth leaving the water brownish and murky. With a flavor of turbid Dr. Pepper, it is a taste that must be acquired. After the villagers got to know us better, several of the cruising wives were allowed to join their husbands at a non-ceremonial kava cocktail party. Even though it is non-alcoholic, this peppery drink has quite a tranquilizing effect. It is easy to see why Fijians are known for being good-natured.

As Bill prepared to make his first official visit, he donned his sulu or wrap-around skirt. This was a sight to behold. Thankfully, he let me take his picture. Otherwise, none of our family or friends back home would have believed it. Bill eventually became comfortable wearing his sulu and even took to wearing it in the big city. Frankly, I thought he looked very handsome. So did the Fijian ladies judging from the smiles on their faces.

Wrapping his skirt around him and taking his mission seriously, as he should, Bill dinghied to the tiny village of Lalati on Bega (pronounced mbenga) to make his presentation to the chief. Women are not allowed at this ceremony and I remained on the boat.

Inviting Bill to join them, they formed a circle and sat cross-legged on the tapa cloth. Presenting the bundle of waka to the chief and hosts, Bill explained why we were there, beginning the custom known as sevu sevu. He was in turn presented with an mbilo (half coconut shell) filled with kava. Clapping once, Bill drained the cup and then everyone clapped three times signifying we were officially welcomed into the village.

Early in the morning of our first Sunday, we returned to the tiny village of about fifty adults and the same number of children. We were greeted warmly and welcomed into their church. The entire service was in Fijian, but we were given a special greeting and message in English. The minister spoke simply and humbly, saying that he wished us safety in our travels. He went on to say that some would think it harmful giving up old traditions for Christianity but they are happier now, remembering the days of cannibalism not too long ago. The church was filled with strong male and female voices harmonizing together. We recognized some of the hymns by their tune and we followed along in the hymnbook, singing the Fijian words with them.

They love to sing, and the deep-throated voices of the men accompanied with the melodic harmony of the women fill the churches. They are caught in the profound emotion of their music as they sing. They sing when they walk and sing when they work.

Fijians attend church three times on Sunday-early morning, afternoon and dusk. The lalo or native ceremonial drum calls the hour of church. With boys on one side and girls on the other, everyone is adorned in their Sunday best-of sulus and shirts with ties or short-sleeved colorful shirts.

Their dark bushy hair is combed and oiled to perfection, forming a natural halo.

A village elder glowers over the children, carrying a long, thin rod. Let one of the boys disturb the Sabbath and he is rapped swiftly on the head. Just the threat of the stick keeps the boys quiet and mannerly.

They recognize the importance of their family and have no economic competition, sharing equally with neighbors and relatives. The old, infirm or widowed never have to worry, and are secure in the knowledge that the village will take care of them. Many times we were asked why our children weren't with us. Trying to explain that they were grown, some married with children of their own, didn't seem sufficient enough reason to them. To the Fijian it was unthinkable to leave behind any family member.

The gardens are individually owned and planted but the life is essentially cooperative. There is an unending food supply. The richness of the soil requires no fertilizer, irrigation or plowing—just weeding and simple planting.

Mountain lakes supply fresh water on some of the islands. The exceptional tasting water on Viti Levu is naturally filtered by artesian wells. Its smooth, creamy flavor contains a high content of silica, believed to help prevent Alzheimer's, among other benefits.

Fijians are very clean, bathing and washing clothes tirelessly. They keep tidy homes and grounds going so far as to sweep the footprints from the sand. Men and women are equally fastidious about their hair, keeping it combed out in a neat frizz. Little children's hair is cut very close to the head— a "buzz"—even on the girls. It would have been hard to tell the boys from the girls except females never wore pants or shorts.

After church, Semi and Lusi invited us to have dinner at their home. As we entered the tidy 15'x15' room, we couldn't help notice that this one room was living room, dining room and bedroom for the entire family of four.

Sitting on the mat-covered floor, a feast of fish was laid out with rourou (like creamed spinach), chicken and noodle soup (fresh and homemade), casaba root, and ota in lolo (watercress boiled in coconut milk—delicious). Fijians don't generally use cutlery, but they brought out spoons in our honor. We enjoyed every bite and didn't even mind shooing away the chickens trying to join the dinner party. When the dishes were cleared, we were invited to "rest," meaning everyone reclines on the mat instead of sits. The door is closed as a sign to the village that there is no longer open house and we lay there chatting for a while. Shortly afterward, we arose to have tea made from lemon leaves.

Everyone here is overwhelmingly hospitable. It is hard to comprehend that these islanders' ancestors were cannibals. As one old Fijian gentleman said "We could be related. My grandfather may have eaten your grandfather." Reflecting on the experience, I couldn't help but think that a hundred years earlier, we could have been their main course instead of their guests.

Fijians love to have their picture taken and we were kept busy as the new village photographers. The Polaroid was put to good use in making a lot of villagers happy. Parents would rush over with their children and proudly pose as dozens of others tried to crowd into the happy family photo. They would show up once to make sure they were in the picture, then run home to get on their finest clothes and show up again for a better one. The only problem we encountered was getting the little babies to smile. They would take one look at our strange white faces and burst out crying.

Another act of Fiji kindness occurred as we went to explore a reef off a nearby, uninhabited island. Making the voyage in our dinghy, we sat on the beach after a snorkel. A group of teenage boys were spear fishing and offered us some fish they had caught moments before. We politely refused, saying that we didn't have any money or anything to trade. Their chaperone spoke to them in their native language and soon the boys were cleaning the fish with the sharp edge of a shell. One of the boys disappeared into the brush with the cleaned fish. Moments later, we were presented with grilled fish on a piece of folded newspaper. Off they ran again, this time returning with coconuts. Lopping off the tops of the coconuts with their machete, they offered us the sweet milk to wash down the fish. As a final course, dessert was the sweet meat of the coconut.

Raising our anchor once again, we moved to the island of Ono and anchored off the village of Naqara. Here is where we would leave our hearts in Fiji.

As soon as Bill finished sevu sevu with the chief, he returned in the dinghy to bring me to shore. The ladies greeted us with gifts of shells and woven mats. I, in return, caused frenzy when I reached into my bag and brought out their gifts—empty plastic bottles. Before coming to Fiji, we asked what kinds of gifts the people most desire and were told that containers of any size or type are highly prized. Rice and flour must be kept dry. These plastic disposables considered a nuisance in the U.S., are valuable commodities in Ono.

Something occurred that really touched me. Instead of grabbing something and keeping it, each lady that received an item passed it to another. The spirit of giving is deeply ingrained in the Fijians. We would experience their generosity many times over before we left.

The first time we entered the village, three-year-old Alfred greeted us. "Bula," he said.

He approached us with his hand held out and repeated "Bula, kai valangi" (Hello, foreign white man).

He was everywhere we looked, running all around the village. Intently studying anyone working, he wanted to be where the action was. Alfred soon became my favorite among the children because of his energy and curiosity.

Our first day there happened to coincide with a special celebration of the attachment of the church roof. The ceremony began with the men drinking kava and the women singing with the children. Laying out mats around the churchyard, we sat with the villagers to enjoy the sights, sounds and smells of this unique event.

A procession slowly moved toward the center of the village led by the head carpenter blowing the haunting sound of the triton shell. Behind him followed all the single women carrying their mats. As the carpenter blew the shell, the women would answer him with a loud yell. Turning quickly, he began to chase the women, each one waving her mat and screaming. When the carpenter caught the one of his choice, he was allowed to "keep" her. Asking what that meant, we were answered with a shrug of the shoulder. It's now just legend, we were told.

Morgan and Jane on *Trinity* joined us in Naqara and our quick stop turned into a two-week stay. The Lucids, avid players of all games, would rekindle our enthusiasm for cribbage and bridge. Every evening we would manage to play some type of game. This is where we would begin an odyssey of playing bridge across the Pacific that would eventually get us in trouble in Vanuatu.

Bill and Morgan became very involved in the ordinary village life by helping to repair outboard motors, rudders and propellers. Almost every day they were asked to help the fishermen whose livelihoods and lives depend on their boats running smoothly. In the evening, they would relax around the kava bowl, sharing ideas and experiences of the different cultures.

Weaving mats is the task of the women. Usually this is done at the end of the day when all other chores are completed and the men are drinking kava. The mats are a very important part of interior decorating. There is very little furniture in a Fijian hut and the mat is utilized for sitting, reclining, and eating. I was interested in learning how the mats were woven and they were pleased to give me lessons. Although there was not enough time to complete a large mat, I did learn how to weave a hat.

The majority of Fijians speak, read and write excellent English. Even in the smallest of villages, education is stressed. We visited one of these little schools and were amazed to see the first-graders able to read eight-letter words in two languages. School supplies are difficult to get. The resourceful teachers improvise with whatever they can collect, such as empty cereal boxes and paper scraps.

The huts in the village are built of bamboo or aluminum, sometimes a combination of both. There are no windows but three of the four sides have doors. When the doors are open, there is "open house" and neighbors come and go as they please, visiting, chatting, and sharing smokes and snacks.

After hearing our glowing radio reports about the diving, Patsy and Chris on *Jalingo* sailed over to join us. The six of us dived and dined together every day.

Fiji diving has anything you could want. Canyons of huge gorgonias in vivid reds and yellows, tunnels decorated with multi-colored soft corals and age-old black coral trees were so plenteous it was impossible to take them in with just one dive. A kaleidoscope of brilliant colors—purple, orange and red dazzled the mind. Huge white mushroom-like coral mixed with multihued crinoids provided a masterpiece for the photo bug. Schools of batfish, amberjack and shimmering schools of silver fish merged with the occasional black-tipped shark. The little tropical fish—damsels, clowns, butterflies, angels, and Moorish idols darted among the anemone and coral formations for protection. They were all here. In fact, you would be hard-pressed to name a Pacific tropical fish that could not be seen in Fijian waters.

Only fifty feet below the surface, tunnels and caves wait for the more adventurous diver. Their walls and roofs are covered with soft corals in every color of the rainbow-shades of red and yellow, purple and maroon. This area is also prolific in fluted and giant clams and other members of the clam family. I collected several nice specimens of spider conchs and scorpion conchs.

Every dive promises a catch for the underwater hunter. The area abounds with species from the delicious coral trout to the big ocean-going Spanish mackerel. For anyone desiring to spear fish, dinner was available. This is truly one of the natural wonders of the world.

Dave, an Aussie living here, offered to take us to his favorite diving hole. He picked us up the next morning with a beer in his hand. By the time we arrived at the dive spot, empty beer cans littered the bottom of the skiff.

We followed him into the water and watched as he speared one fish after another attracting a few small sharks. Bill and I followed him as he dove deeper and deeper. Bill motioned to me and pointed to his depth gauge. It read one hundred and eighty-five feet. I wasn't sure how long we had been down, but I pointed to the boat. Bill nodded and we started up. Stopping at the twenty-foot level, we held onto the anchor line and decompressed. Back in the boat, we worried about Dave staying at such a depth for so long. After what seemed like too long a time for a safe dive, Dave popped up and casually threw a bag full of fresh catch into the skiff.

"Are you okay?" Bill asked.

"Sure, mate. Except I had to leave behind a few big ones. Those pesky sharks were getting a little too cheeky."

It was time to leave Ono. As we dinghied to shore for the last time, there on the beach waiting, were father Pauli, daughters Aggie and Marica and many others. With pencils and toys for the children, we thanked them and said our good-byes. Returning to *Pegaso*, we were busy raising the anchor and heard voices. There they were, the family looking up at us from their skiff. Their faces reflecting the sorrow of good-byes. In their hands was a gift of an heirloom tapa cloth made by the grandmother. How fitting and so in keeping with the character of the folks we came to know and love. They did not want to owe us anything. They needed to be the last to give. Pauli gave a little speech. All I heard were the words "when you return to our island." And we knew we would never see them again…and that they knew it also.

Trinity and *Pegaso* literally sailed off into the sunset together. There was still time left to enjoy more of Fiji and we were eager to share the experience. We looked forward to a future with islands to see, dives to make and bridge to play.

It was a bumpy overnight sail to the island of Gnau (pronounced now). Our arrival needed to be perfectly timed in the morning to have the sunlight at our backs and expose the dangerous reef surrounding the island. Not able at first to clearly distinguish the safe entry to the island, the two boats lingered outside the reef.

After several exchanges on the radio with *Trinity* about strategy, Bill climbed the mizzen and straddled the spreader. Shouting down from his perch where to steer, I blindly followed his instructions with *Trinity* close behind, and we safely passed through the narrow entrance to Gnau. Again anchored in crystal clear azure water, the same scenario of the previous islands played for us.

On this occasion our host was Sowani, arriving to invite all of us to a "lovo" or earth-oven barbecue in honor of our visit. They generously provided the suckling pig baked in the ground to delicate perfection with baked fresh coconut for dessert. "What could we bring?" we asked. Only matches to light the fire and salt, items hard to preserve in humid Fiji.

Over and over, the extraordinary hospitality of the Fijians touched our hearts. It was a rare privilege to live among these people. Soon we would leave for Vanuatu with the excitement of discovering something new and gratitude for the privilege of knowing these islands.

11
Vanuatu and Things My Husband Didn't Want Me To Write Home About

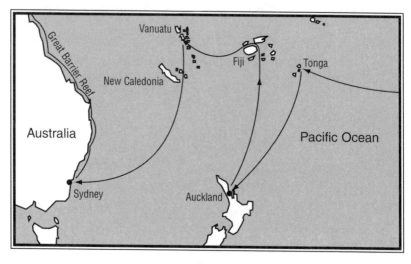

There are some things that happen while cruising that you're ashamed to admit. A captain letting his boat float away would easily come under that category. There we were in a gorgeous little anchorage in Vanuatu anchored at the base of a volcano majestically dominating the view. We could have been diving. We could have been hiking. We could have been enjoying the night sky awash with the brilliant light emanating from the volcano. But, we were playing bridge with Morgan and Jane on board *Trinity*. All day and into the night. And while Bill and I were "off watch" *Pegaso* decided to leave without us.

Earlier that same day, we entered the small bay and I let go the anchor. As Bill had done hundreds of times before, he put the engine in reverse so the anchor would dig in and hold tightly. Instead it skipped over the bottom. Using the electric windlass, I brought the anchor up and we tried again. This time it went down in a different location. Still it didn't hold. For the third time, we started all over again. Anchor up, drop it down again. The anchor was trying to tell us it didn't like the lava rock bottom. After the fourth try, Bill finally thought it grabbed and it appeared as though we were in.

Before arriving here, we heard warnings that a dinghy was stolen in this bay. The owner of the dinghy suspected the locals of the theft. Despite the rumor, our enthusiasm to visit wasn't dampened. We presumed the most likely event was the captain just didn't tie his dinghy securely and it drifted away. The locals were aware that the yachties wouldn't come if they felt it wasn't a safe place to be. They didn't want the yachties to take their dollars elsewhere so they set up their own sentinel on the beach. Lucky for us. If they hadn't, *Pegaso* might still be floating around the Pacific by herself.

We were still playing bridge around nine in the evening. A loud knock on the hull stopped us but only momentarily. Since there were no other cruisers in the area, the four of us assumed that it was one of the natives paying a visit at this late hour. Barely looking up from our cards, we decided to ignore the visitor because of another warning we received. This one from the government: It is forbidden to give alcohol to the citizens. Assuming that whoever was knocking would be asking for liquor, we decided not to answer and went back to our game. The knocking persisted, only this time louder and more determined than before. This made us think that we'd better answer if we wanted to get rid of him, since it didn't appear he was anxious to go away. Morgan stuck his head up out of the passageway.

"Yes? What can we do for you?"

Pointing out to sea he said, "Was two boats, now one."

At first, I didn't get it. But Morgan and Bill understood well. *Pegaso* was gone. Everyone sprang up the steps and on deck. As our eyes began to adjust to the darkness, we could barely see *Pegaso*'s anchor light at the top of the mast several miles away. Surely it couldn't be. But it was.

Bill hastened to untie our dinghy. I begged him not to go after *Pegaso*. I knew the small outboard motor was almost empty. I was positive he would run out of gas and be carried out to sea. *Pegaso* would be easy to find but I knew we'd never find Bill.

I couldn't stop him. Bill was heading into the darkness towards the mast light miles away. All I could do was plead with him. "Don't go. Please, don't go."

It was a futile effort on my part. He was a man on a mission and just ignored me. In the meantime, Morgan and Jane began to lift *Trinity*'s anchor and prepared to follow Bill.

The two men who brought us the news were still onboard and wanted to go with us. Waving their arms in the air "Please, please let us go. Let us go," they begged.

And I was still running around waving my arms in the air, yelling at Bill into the empty darkness "Don't go. Don't go."

Reluctantly, Morgan allowed them to tie their pontoon boat to *Trinity*'s stern. We traveled no more than a few hundred yards when the fragile pontoon boat began to break into pieces and drift away. Our passengers became overwrought.

"Don't go. Don't go." one wailed at Morgan. Now he was on my side.

"Oh, my God, my father's going to kill me," sobbed this forty-something man.

"He doesn't know I took the boat. I didn't ask permission and now it's all broken. What am I going to do?"

While this was happening Bill managed to successfully reach *Pegaso*. Once onboard, he radioed back to us that everything was under control and he was returning to the anchorage. What a relief.

Knowing all was safe aboard *Pegaso*, we concentrated our efforts in finding the wreckage of the pontoon in the darkness. By the next day, each piece was recovered and the entire boat eventually repaired.

Our two new friends visited us in the morning aboard *Trinity*. After learning that Morgan was a doctor, he seized on the opportunity to have Morgan tend to a festering sore on his leg. When Morgan was finished bandaging the area, the patient turned to me and said, "Aren't you glad we were on the beach last night?"

"Yes, I am. Thank you very much for warning us." I said.

"What I mean is aren't you very glad we were there on the beach." He emphasized the "very." I finally got it.

"Oh, yes. Yes, we are very glad." I could see he was relieved he didn't have to explain further. "What can we do to show our appreciation?" I asked him.

His eyes lit up and he didn't hesitate. "Got any Scotch?"

Just southwest of Vanuatu lies New Caledonia, a French territory island. We timed our arrival just right so we could pass the treacherous reefs during the day. There is an unusual sight in the town square. Flying right next to the French flag is the American flag and a large memorial to our troops. The French citizens of New Cal are still paying tribute to the American service men of World War II for liberating them from the Japanese. When anyone learned that we were Americans, they never failed to express their gratitude for something that happened almost fifty years ago.

We stayed only a month but Bill's natural ability to make friends through tennis paid off. One day he showed up at the boat with a very interesting French Vietnamese, Lan Ma-Kim.

Lan told us his story.

"I escaped from Vietnam when I was in my early twenties. I left on a refugee boat. It very crowded and many people die of sickness. I finally get to France and then to Paris and I reunite with my father and mother. I meet my wife there who is doctor. It is always my dream to make the best *foie gras* in the world. We come here to raise geese and make my fortune."

Lan and Gaetan have twin teenage sons, Rio and Branco. "Have you heard of the Rio Branco River in Brazil?" he asked us. "I always like the name and say that one day I have two sons and name them after the river."

Lan continued. "One day the Chinooks—that's what we call the natives—got mad that I am here. I see a big group of them coming. They come to burn down my house and kill my geese. I go out to meet them and I tell them, first you have to kill me. Then you kill my geese."

The last we heard of Lan he was still struggling to make a success of his goose farm.

The day we left, a group of our new friends came to bid us adieu. Jean Claude, the owner of our favorite restaurant, brought a lei. He placed the colorful circle of flowers around Bill's neck and planted a kiss on each cheek, and a third, "one extra for good luck". Another adieu. We sailed away to the Land of Oz ready for civilization again. Australia, here we come.

12

Australia

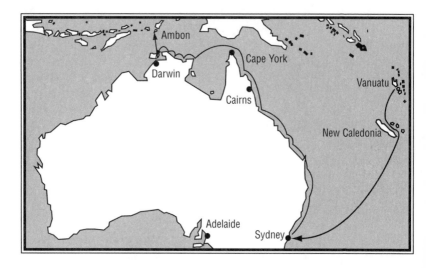

We sailed into the bustling Sydney harbor bringing to an end our uneventful five-day sail from New Caledonia. Rounding the corner inside the harbor, we got our first glimpse of the famous Sydney Opera House impressively perched beside the busy waterways. It was a Sunday afternoon and there was total mayhem in the harbor. Hundreds of serious racers trying to make their courses forced us to dodge in and out of the endless path of sails as we made our way to Rushcutter's Bay Marina, our home for the next six months.

Sydney has the charm of San Francisco and the energy of New York City. Any of the charming suburbs are easily accessible by the subway-train (perfectly safe), water ferry, and bus or by simply walking.

The hub of activity centers on the harbor, with its wholesome environment. Families stroll the walkways enjoying the fresh ocean breeze and open-air restaurants. Clowns amuse the children. Buskers or street entertainers anticipating a donation delight the crowds. Thousands come with blankets to sit on the ground and watch opera performed under the stars.

After nine months spent on islands, we were grateful to be in the "civilized" world again. Once we consumed every play, concert, movie and museum with the appetite of starving men, it was time to get acquainted with the real Australia.

Leaving *Pegaso* in Sydney, we began our tour via air. Big cities are the same all over the world, however, Australia's big cities seemed to be safer and cleaner by comparison. Flying to Melbourne, we attended the Australian Open in their grand new tennis stadium. In Adelaide, Bill entered and was allowed to play in the Australian National Seniors Tournament. From there, we flew to Hobart, Tasmania, rented a car, toured the island and returned to Sydney.

In the summer of January Down Under, bushfires broke out surrounding Sydney. The hot dry weather and the wind out of the northwest pushed the fires uphill and down. As the highly flammable eucalyptus trees burned out of control, thousands of homes were threatened and hundreds destroyed. The winds gusted and the fires roared through the treetops traveling at forty miles an hour or more.

Smoke filled the air and the haze was so thick the days looked like nights. At night, the fires reflected off the haze making the days and nights indistinguishable from each other. Visibility was less than three hundred feet and the airport and roads were closed. Officials advised people to stay indoors out of the smog and suffocating heat of over one hundred degree temperatures.

Even though we were in a harbor surrounded by water there was still concern for everyone's safety. Burning rubbish was known to fly across hundreds of yards and could easily set fire to the sails. We waited for days prepared to motor out of the harbor at a moment's notice.

At last, the winds subsided and cooler and moister weather moved in and the worst seemed to be over. Over one million acres burned and four lives were lost. Someone said fire is a good servant, a bad master, a worse friend and a cruel enemy.

We were beginning to miss the family again and it was time to fly home for a visit. As long as we were going to fly halfway around the world, why not just keep going all the way around? So that is what we did. With a layover in San Francisco to visit son, Burtt, we continued to Palm Beach, Florida to visit both our mothers. My mother, never one to turn down an opportunity, packed her bags and joined us from there. Morgan and Jane met us for a brief stay in London and the five of us continued on to Zimbabwe for a safari and canoe trip down the Zambezi River. After an exciting two weeks in Africa, we all returned to Sydney. Whew, that's one way to pass the time in Australia.

It was time to move north, destination Darwin. Three thousand miles of sailing. One week after returning from our round-the-world flight, we sailed out of Sydney Harbor. With a lengthy trip ahead of us, we allocated three months to cruise it in comfort and give us enough time to enjoy the Great Barrier Reef and Whitsunday Islands. It was to be a leisurely cruise for us. Little did we know that this would be a tragic season for some of our other cruising friends.

It began early in April. There were warnings of winds up to twenty-five knots, but from past experience we knew *Pegaso* could handle it. Bill chose to stay close to the coastline because the offshore currents opposing the winds can cause adverse conditions. We were having a great sail, but not far from us Carl and Christine on *Blue Swan* were further offshore and having a different experience.

We listened to Carl's radio report of strong winds and high seas. As the hours ticked away, they decided to heave to—setting their sails in a way that allowed them to sit tight in one spot and wait out the storm. Tension mounting, they bounced around for two days and kept the rest of us informed of their well being. Then, a rogue wave caught them broadside and they did a complete roll.

Blue Swan sustained extensive damage. Above deck, the mast and all stanchions, stays, and lifelines were wiped out. Below deck, anything not bolted down went flying through the air—canned food, bottles, pots and pans, books, tools and heavy boat batteries stored in the bilge. Carl and Christine were seriously injured with broken bones and internal injuries and were airlifted to Coff's Harbor Hospital. *Blue Swan* was towed into port. But, with their unconquerable spirits, they will be back on the high seas soon.

Doug on *Bright Star* was not so lucky. Doug and Fran overstayed their visa and were told to leave by the Australian authorities. At least that is how they reported it on the radio. Requesting a stay because Doug was under a doctor's care and not well enough to sail, they were refused. So they took on an inexperienced crewmember and left for New Caledonia. Arriving four days later at night, Doug decided to go through the pass between the reefs instead of waiting for the light of morning. Tired and in poor health, he needed some rest. This turned out to be a fatal decision. They hit the reef and Doug was thrown overboard by the impact. The last thing Fran heard him say was "I'm okay. I'm here." The crewman told her to wait below. She refused to abandon ship until he told her that Doug was safe. When she climbed into the enclosed lifeboat, Doug was not there. The French Coast Guard was alerted and came to their rescue. They searched for days and never found Doug.

There were fourteen others who met a similar or worse fate that same year. The area offshore Australia to New Zealand and north to Fiji could be labeled the "Devil's Triangle of the South Pacific" because of its unpredictable weather and seas. Every seaman pays close attention to the weather reports, but even so, unexpected storms hit without warning and catch sailors off guard. We are not better sailors than the others, just more fortunate.

We stopped at almost every major port on the northeast coast of Australia, playing golf along the way and enjoying the sunny weather. Gold Coast looked exactly like south Florida. Even the local signs pointed to cities with familiar names like Palm Beach and Miami.

Sailing inside the Great Barrier Reef is perfection, protected and calm with a breeze always from the southeast. Diving at the Great Barrier Reef is decent. The Cod Hole at Lizard Island is among the best in Australia. Its name describes it aptly with 800-pound grouper-type fish that will eat from your hand.

Another good dive spot is the 104-year-old *Quetta* wreck, lying in a remote area off Cape York, at the most northern point of Australia. Declared a historic shipwreck in 1981, very few people make the effort to go there because it is so isolated. The sea life is abundant and not frightened by intruders such as us. As we dropped into the water, four gigantic manta rays didn't seem at all perturbed that we were there.

Gove is about three hundred fifty miles away. To get there is a straight shot from Cape York southwest across the top of the Gulf of Carpentaria. This is where we had our rendezvous with a whale.

Everything happens at night, but truthfully, it was late at night. We were under way with slightly choppy seas and winds of thirty knots. *Pegaso* sailed along comfortably at ten knots. Bill was on watch and heard the sound of a whale's sonar coming through the hull. By now these sounds were becoming familiar to us and he knew immediately there was a whale in the vicinity.

His first reaction was "Oh, good…a whale" and he went above to admire this magnificent creature of the sea. The whale started to nudge *Pegaso*. That was a bad sign. It meant that either we angered him by invading his territory or disturbing his family, or that he was attracted to our hull and had love on his mind. In any case, we were flirting with a possibly dangerous situation.

The whale continued to bump *Pegaso*. Just as Bill was getting ready to wake me and tell me to put on a life vest, a jarring impact lifted forty-five tons of *Pegaso* out of the water. And that was that. For some reason the whale lost interest and disappeared into the night. Maybe he decided *Pegaso* wasn't going to respond to his amorous intentions or didn't pose any threat to his family or territory. Nevertheless, the whale was gone. And I slept through the whole thing.

The town of Gove is at the uppermost tip of Australia. Except for a few Aborigines the entire population is made up of family and employees of the only large business in town, a bauxite mine. Beautiful homes sit on the ocean dunes overlooking wide beaches of clean white sand. But we soon discovered why there wasn't even a footprint on the sand—salt-water crocodiles.

"Don't even think about walking on the beach," a local told us.

"They'll get you for sure. Yip, they can run faster than a racehorse on a straight path."

"You know, without the crocodiles, this would be heaven on earth—if it weren't for the other things in the water that could kill you."

"Kill you?" I said, stressing the kill. He got my attention.

"Yep. Six."

"First, there's the crocs. And if they don't get you, the great white sharks will. There's the yellow-bellied sea snake. Yip, no known antivenom for that one. Then you've got the stonefish that carries a mean stinger if you step on it. And, oh yes, the box jellyfish. Big as a bucket and deadly. It'll kill you in minutes. Oh, I almost forgot the blue-ringed octopus. If that one bites you, you will be paralyzed and die soon. Just don't pick it up."

"No worries, Mate," we said. It's no wonder the Northern Territory is still undeveloped.

Todd, on Christmas break from Ohio State, joined us in Gove. Bill thought Todd would enjoy himself more around some other young people. So we joined the "Over The Top" (of Australia) regatta from Gove to Darwin. Twenty-five boats participated in the rally and Todd seized an opportunity to see the fun part of life at sea. It was Todd's first real cruising experience and he adapted immediately.

Aborigines declared the area between Gove and Darwin closed to travelers. This is traditional land that was conferred to them forty years ago, but they granted our group a special permit to anchor along the way in specific areas. Visits with the indigenous people were organized and they knew we were coming.

The Aborigines are very shy people. They consider it rude to ask questions and, therefore, don't like to have questions asked of them. A spokesman for the group, usually the chief, was chosen to receive the group at each anchorage. The others would join us for barbecue on the beach, but they kept to themselves. If we tried to converse, they would look at the ground and smile shyly, but not answer.

The Aborigines we met keep their old ways and customs. As the authentic free spirit, if they want to work, they work. If they don't want to work, they go on "walkabout" and head for the bush land. They are innately intelligent about ecology and farming, often able to draw food from sandy soil but mostly eating the wild yams and berries.

There is a strong family union among them. The children attend school, although they are not forced to go. There are no do's or don'ts, no rules. Mothers don't discipline their children in any way. Whatever they want to do is fine. If a person does something especially wrong, he is brought before a tribunal and given a lecture by the elders, which could last all day long, depending on the severity of the offense.

Each day, as we sailed from point to point, there was a fishing contest among the cruisers. Dropping a hook off the stern always produced a tuna or mackerel. At night the catch was brought to the beach and grilled over a fire to be shared by everyone, including our Aboriginal hosts.

With a twenty-foot tide, it was necessary to drag our heavy inflatable dinghies to high ground to keep them from being washed away. Those who failed to do so lost their only means of transportation to shore.

Entertainment was provided by the yachties. Guitars were brought out and we sang songs together around the fire. The Americans sang along to

"Waltzing Matilda," the Australians joined in when we sang "Yankee Doodle," while the Swiss and Germans performed their favorite familiar songs. The following evening, there was a bottle of champagne for whoever could tell the best "rippin' yarn". I had to ask what that was. "Just a good story, mate" was the answer.

After the evening's festivities were ended and the fires were dying, we would all head back to our own boats. No one needed a flashlight because the phosphorescence in the wet sand formed perfectly illuminated footprints. Each step caused little sparks to land on top of our bare feet giving new meaning to flashy shoes. When the outboard motors were started the whole fleet of dinghies lit up as though we were in a Hollywood grand opening. We never experienced this much phosphorescence anywhere else in the world.

Todd yacht-hopped and made a few passages with Rob, a young Aussie. Rob bought *Misha* in England and sailed his twenty-seven foot, thirty year-old Fedship back to Australia. The only chart Rob had was a map of the world. That would be unthinkable to most sailors.

After finally arriving in Darwin, it was time to stock up again for the next leg of our trip through Indonesia. Enjoying the convoy experience helped us decide to join another rally that would take us to Ambon in Indonesia, almost 600 miles north. Not only would we share our trip with the same fun group of cruisers, but again the organizers of the rally would provide all the paperwork and save us all the bureaucratic hassles.

In late July, we left Darwin with seventy-four other boats participating in the Darwin to Ambon Race. At night, the sea glistened with phosphorescence that matched the steel gray color of the sky. It gave the ghostly appearance of having no horizon—as though there was no beginning and no end to the world.

Pegaso was the first of our division to cross over the finish line and into Ambon harbor about two o'clock in the morning. Two boats were already tied stern-to at the wharf. A local was standing on the edge waving a flashlight at us. "Over here. Back in over here." Instinct told Bill not to go there, "Are you sure it's okay?"

"Yes, no problem."

We heard a big crunch and stopped dead in the water. The rudder hit and the inch thick stainless steel rod snapped in half. It was the hydraulic ram that turned the rudder. The steering was gone. The "dockmaster" turned out to be the town drunk. He was nowhere to be found after that.

Pegaso had plenty of spare parts. We had two of everything on board. Bill got out the spare rod and in ten minutes we were safely tied to the wall.

It was our first experience in southeast Asia, and we were going to learn a few lessons about dealing with different manners and customs.

13
Indonesia

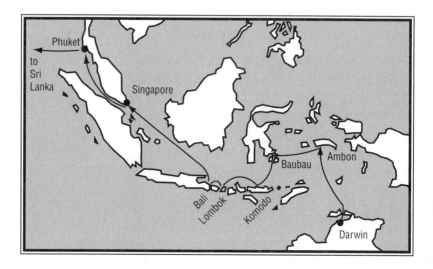

Another common question asked us is "Did you ever have problems with pirates?"

Before we began our odyssey, the problem of pirates seemed very remote to us. A little research had Bill thinking that pirates are only interested in large freighters with large amounts of cash on board. What would they want with a little sailboat? But the closer we got to Indonesia, the more we heard about piracy in that area. Understandably nervous, Bill began to think that somewhere there might be a pirate-in-training and he might want to practice his trade on some of us. After meeting Don and Cathy on *Kelolo* we were even more wary.

Shortly after arriving in Ambon, Don and Cathy invited four cruising couples to their boat.

"What I am about to tell you is very hard for us to talk about." Don began. "But I have to explain why we are asking if you will buddy-boat with us."

"About a year ago, we were cruising in New Guinea. Three men came to the boat and offered to buy our twenty-year-old daughter. We thought it was amusing and we were polite but turned them away. That night they returned to the boat to kidnap our daughter but couldn't find her. Her cabin had a separate outside entrance. They couldn't figure that out and thought she wasn't on board. They tied up Cathy and me and threatened us all night. In front of us, they discussed how they would rape Cathy, kill us both and dispose of our bodies. We spoke calmly to them, and convinced them not to harm us. Before the sun came up, they left. It was very traumatic for us and we considered the possibility of quitting cruising. I think you will understand now why we are not comfortable cruising these waters alone and hope you will let us join you." There was no question what everyone would say. This sweet and gentle couple had lived through a horrible nightmare. From then on, the five cruising yachts remained together for the next three thousand miles throughout Indonesia.

With us were Lorraine and Brian on *Mara*, a catamaran from Australia, Mike and Jean with crew members Andrew and Leslie on *Risky Business* from Australia, and Al and Katharine Overton on *Ethereal* from California.

We began by sailing around the island of Ambon. Although just one of 13,677 islands in Indonesia and a mere dot on the map, it is home to 250,000 people. Ambon is different from most of the other Indonesian islands in that the people practice Christianity and are influenced by former Dutch rule.

The people of Ambon resemble the very dark-skinned, bushy-haired neighbors in nearby New Guinea. As we sailed further west, the people became lighter skinned, with straight hair, and Muslim. Even further west, they took on an oriental look and were mostly Hindu. We were in Indonesia, stretching across 3,200 miles of sea, but it hardly seemed like it at times with the differences in the people and culture.

Although there are over three hundred different languages, the common language is Bahasa. Very little English is spoken and Bill did an admirable job of becoming conversational in Bahasa, gaining a great deal of appreciation from the Indonesians for his efforts.

The cruising grounds of Indonesia were some of the most pleasant that we encountered. In the protected waters, there was always a calm sea followed by a light breeze. Even the night passages became enjoyable. With a full moon before us casting its light on the water, I could envision sailing down a yellow brick road. The only complaint could be that sometimes there wasn't enough wind.

Dodging the hundreds of fishermen and their nets could be bothersome. But they were always aware of us and would shine their dim kerosene lights our way to let us know they saw us coming. Considering that we were the invaders into their territory, we thought they were exceptionally considerate.

On one particular night passage through the Strait of Malaca, an amusing thing occurred. The wind completely died and we were becalmed. For several hours we sat in one spot with the knot meter reading 00.0. We were entered in a friendly race and if we turned on our engine we would have to withdraw. Bill turned to me and said, "We're moving backwards."

He was right. But how could that be? There was no current. No wind. Our sails were still and yet we were moving backwards?

Looking around, we saw the lights of a Malaysian fishing boat about a mile away. And Bill figured it out. We were caught in his net and he was dragging us backward. It was a good thing the engine wasn't running. Both the fisherman and we would have been in a real predicament. About five minutes later, the fisherman must have guessed what was tugging at his nets, because the net fell off our keel and we were free.

We stopped at many islands as we worked our way west. Some of the islands had not had visitors for years. At each island, we could always expect the same welcome.

"Hello, Meester." It didn't matter whether they were addressing male or female, it was always "mister." It was the only English they knew. There were always great big smiles from the older inhabitants and cries of terror from the babies. Each visit would draw a crowd consisting of nearly the whole village. Children ran up, touched our skin and checked their fingers to see if the white color had come off, then ran back to Mommy laughing.

On one occasion, an old lady approached me and started playing with the buttons on my shirt. I thought she just wanted to see how they worked and didn't resist until I detected that she was trying to undress me so she could have my shirt. The next day I traded her the shirt for a few shells.

Curious locals in their dugouts or perahus constantly surrounded our boat. It was a real struggle to politely keep them off. The minute we turned our back, they would crawl on board to visit or just to look. They were perfectly happy just to sit and watch us do our chores. With an array of noses pressed up against the galley windows peering at me, I would go about my chores, baking bread or preparing meals. Bill would usually sit in the cockpit with his Bahasa-English dictionary and attempt to converse. Their lovely dispositions, constant smiling and pleasantness made it extremely difficult to ask them to leave.

About 80% of the islands are Muslim. Even in a small village, it was not unusual to see several large mosques. I couldn't help but notice that these temples always seemed to occupy the prime waterfront property. We became accustomed to the loudspeakers calling the faithful to prayer four times a day. The five a.m. call seemed to be the loudest, of course.

Often I took my shell book with me to the villages to point out some shells that I was particularly interested in. It worked. We all became deluged with helpful natives overwhelming us with all types of shells. Big shells, little shells, new shells, old shells, clean shells, but mostly dirty shells. There were certain unwanted occupants in each of the shells, ranging from mollusks to roaches, requiring us to thoroughly soak and clean each one before taking them on board our vessels. Everyone went home with armloads of shells.

Particularly memorable is Buru, an island formerly used as a prison for political dissidents. Outsiders were only recently allowed to stop there. The villagers spotted us coming and the whole village lined up along the road and followed us everywhere. Before we entered the tiny bay and dropped our anchor, we could hear the excited voices of the people shouting our arrival. It was a long time since any outsiders had visited, and never a white person.

We were escorted through the brush to their most important spot on the island, the water hole. With great pride, their leader pointed to the muddy water. Assuming he was offering us the opportunity to fill our boats, we did our best to explain that we were grateful for the offer but didn't need any water. When we returned to the village, a young boy was ordered up one of the many coconut trees and cut down a half dozen green coconuts. On the spot, they were hacked open with machetes and we drank the milk and ate the gelatinous, sweet meat of the immature fruit.

There was no doctor or medicine on the tiny island. The people looked to us for relief of various ailments. Many times in our travels this occurred. Most yachts carried a full supply of medical supplies: oral antibiotics, medication for urinary tract infections, malaria medication, pain medication of all strengths, and much more. We even carried tanks of oxygen in preparation for a case of the bends and inflatable splints in case of a broken arm or leg. We kept scalpels and morphine in case we found it necessary to perform surgery, which, I guess was pretty silly because neither one of us would be capable. We heard of one unlucky woman whose husband had to perform an appendectomy while following the instructions of a surgeon on the radio. Fortunately, Bill already had his appendix removed when he was young. What happened to her was always in the back of my mind. We were prepared for almost any type of medical emergency, but that would be a sailor's nightmare. Particularly this sailor.

Forewarned not to give natives oral medication of any kind because they would take the whole treatment at once, it was frustrating to see so many suffering people and not be able to help—not even give them a bottle of aspirin.

Particularly, I remember a young pregnant woman on Buru. Her husband stopped us as we walked through the village. Using sign language and our Bahasa dictionary we were able to understand that she was suffering from a very bad urinary tract infection. Even though we had the proper medicine for her problem, the only advice we were able to give her was to drink plenty of water.

Later, four of the older men paddled out to *Pegaso* with an offering of three eggs. Knowing that eggs are a delicacy to them, I was ashamed to take them. We already had plenty. Nevertheless, it was a very touching gift and the eggs had to be accepted so as not to offend them. In return, we gave them much-desired T-shirts, and the always-coveted empty plastic containers for their wives. Even though T-shirts were a favorite gift, the Buru men did have limitations. One of those we gave away was pink. When I handed it to a man, he promptly passed it on to a young boy. Even the poorest fisherman in Indonesia wouldn't wear pink. The young boy didn't look too happy with it either.

Offering them coffee to drink, I set the cockpit table as I would for anyone—with the usual sugar and milk in small ceramic pitchers. I was surprised to see one of the men pick up a spoon and ladle large amounts of sugar into the pitcher of milk. He then picked up the small pitcher and began to drink from it. My mistake, of course. Here when coffee is served the milk and sugar have already been added. Milk is served as a beverage and he naturally assumed that was what it was for.

Forewarned not to show the bottoms of our feet or the bottoms of our shoes because it is considered rude, we made a special effort not to cross our legs. Patting the children's heads was considered perilous to the child and just not done. These were things that took concentration to remember not to do.

But for them to offer their left hand to someone was equally as wrong. Here, as in many countries, the right hand is for eating and the left hand is for personal hygiene. A mischievous eight year-old was told to shake hands and, with a twinkle in his eye, he offered me his left hand. Daddy grunted and scowled and he quickly withdrew it and stuck out his right hand instead.

We sailed down through the Buton Straits of Sulawesi, home of the once-feared local pirates named the Bugis. The word bogeyman was derived from the frightful tales told about the Bugis. According to our traveler's guide, as early as the 1800's, parents would warn children not to misbehave or else the bogeymen might get them. As soon as I learned this little tidbit of history, I had an urge to apologize to my sister, Carmen, for doing the same thing to her when we were kids.

The Bugis' chief business nowadays is boat building. They build boats without plans, using traditional tools and simple handsaws. These wooden boats are replicas of the Western schooners of the 1800s. Two-inch ironwood pegs hold the wooden planks together. They are full-keeled with a draft of about four feet. These craft are mainly used as transport vessels and with a low freeboard and fully loaded, the decks are often awash.

On the island of Baubau, in the village of Sulaa, every female, from very young girls to very old ladies, has a loom. Sitting beneath the stilted houses, they weave as long as the sun is shining. As Katharine and I crouched beneath the house to watch, we drew a crowd of ladies. We came to observe and became the observed. The ladies started to talk among themselves, looking at us and laughing. We asked the local teacher, the only one who spoke English, what were they saying. "They are laughing at your noses," was his answer.

"Our noses? Why?"

"Because they are long and pointed."

Well, everyone is entitled to his opinion.

We celebrated my fiftieth birthday on the island of Baubau with a party aboard *Pegaso*. *Risky Business* arrived with birthday hats. *Kelolo* and *Mara* brought big, brightly decorated balloons. Katharine on *Ethereal* asked me what kind of cake I wanted. I put in an order for white cake with chocolate frosting then jokingly added "and Haagen Daz vanilla ice cream." She knew I was kidding. We hadn't seen that since we left the U.S. Katharine brought the cake and homemade ice cream, too. It was so delicious, I couldn't tell the difference between that and my favorite H.D. It was my most memorable birthday.

For good reason, we anchored right over a wall filled with lobster on Lantiagana in the Tiger Islands. Diving at forty feet and staying down for an hour allowed us to gather a sumptuous dinner for the fleet. Mike and Jean are dive masters and carry a compressor to fill air tanks. It was a symbiotic relationship. We provided water for them and they provided air for us. It was our first good dive in Indonesia. Most of the reefs are dead and look like a sea of dried bones. The fishermen practice what they call "loud" fishing—fishing with dynamite. As a result, they have destroyed the good dive spots and most of our diving/snorkeling was disappointing.

Komodo and Rinca Islands are the only two islands in the world that can claim to be home to the Komodo dragon. The Komodo dragon is an enormous monitor lizard that can grow to ten feet and weigh over three hundred twenty-five pounds. The reptiles eat deer, pigs and their own young. It can smell a meal through its tongue eight miles away. They have been known to eat water buffalo and even, reportedly, two unlucky tourists. In 1979, a Swiss baron wandered off the trail and all that was found was his camera case and bloody shirt.

On Komodo, our guide led the tour with a long, forked stick on a forty minute walk through the bush to a corral for people. There, we were closed in for our safety where we could observe the dragons up close. Up until two weeks before we arrived, the lizards were fed a whole goat. They ceased this practice saying the lizards were getting lazy. We counted over twenty lizards near the compound waiting to be fed. Apparently, they didn't get the message the handouts were over.

Raising the anchor early one morning on Lombok, we looked up to see a huge, gray cloud rising on the island. Mount Baru was erupting. Putting the throttle up to full speed, we tried to get out of the area as fast as we were able. Soon every one of us was covered with fine black sand. Slowly, the whole sky turned gray and the sun faded. It was only a minor inconvenience and thankfully, none of the islanders were harmed. Months later, we were still trying to get rid of volcanic ash.

The five yachts continued on together and dropped anchor off a small island consisting of a few lean-tos used by the Bugi fishermen as an overnight stop. This was one of those times when there was safety in numbers. These were a rough group of men.

Bill and I decided that we would go to the island to explore a little and look for shells. About twenty Bugis saw us coming and approached us aggressively led by a younger, rugged man.

Trying to be friendly, we stopped and Bill spoke a few words of Bahasa. The leader of the group was a bully and decided he would assert himself. Reaching over, he snatched Bill's baseball cap from the top of his head and placed it on his own, then turned around to his friends to get their approval. The group howled with laughter and egged him on.

It wasn't so much the act that warned us. It was the look in his eyes. They were hollow, dead eyes, almost as though there was no soul in there. Bill felt a sense of foreboding and gently took me by the hand. We turned and left as they taunted and laughed.

Later, gathered together on board *Risky Business* for one of our potluck dinners, we could see the men making their way towards us under sail in their big wooden perahu. After several short tacks, they pulled alongside and the bully jumped on board ready to confront the group. Bill knew this was a situation that was very delicate and we didn't want any confrontations with these men. Bill was able to talk them into leaving peacefully but it was obvious they were not pleased. Shortly after, we moved to another anchorage far away.

Ah, Bali. What can I possibly say about Bali that hasn't already been said. "Magical" is the word most often used. And it is.

In spite of the overpopulation of tourists (two million per year), it's easy to get lost in the wonder of its beauty. Twenty thousand Hindu temples flourish, some as old as nine hundred years. Rice fields terrace the hillsides forming a lush green panorama. Tropical jungles harbor monkeys. Each village specializes in certain crafts—woodcarving, batik, pottery, gold and silver. At night, there are festivals with dance, drama and music.

But it was the rice paddies that produced the most prominent image. Very narrow paths with irrigation ditches on either side surrounded them. The ground would give way at times while walking along them and a foot could easily end up in the water.

Our buddy-boating team continued to keep close together during this trip because of more reports of piracy in the area. I started to get paranoid about pirates coming on board at night. Even as I was alone on watch at night, I would sometimes feel that they were following us, ready to come alongside and board. But I knew I was being ridiculous. Or was I?

Tim and Ann on *Sunrise* recounted their story to us one evening. "We were sailing along in the Straits of Malaca at night. Ann was on watch alone. She looked up and there was a man standing in the cockpit. She didn't even hear a noise. When she screamed, I came running up just in time to see him jump overboard. Next we heard an outboard motor crank up and the boat took off."

I was glad that when Tim and Ann told us their story, we were already out of that part of the world.

When I look back on our two months in Indonesia, there are some things that I'll never forget. The permanent smiles of the people. The fiery, red sunsets. The call to prayer. A volcano's minor eruption. The bright blue sails of the little perahus. The new taste of unfamiliar fruits. Shopping in Bali. And pirates—whether real or imaginary.

129

14
Singapore to The Suez Canal

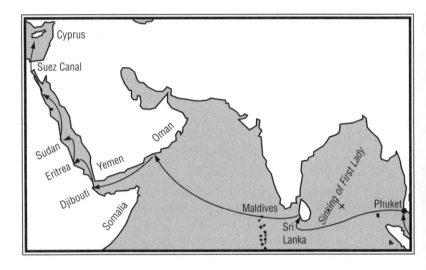

We crossed the equator back into the northern hemisphere and made our way toward Singapore. It took us sixteen days of dayhops and only two overnighters. Our journey was mostly motor sailing in nice weather with the hatches open.

Entering Singapore Harbor, we were surrounded by gigantic super-tankers. The radar screen resembled a bad case of chicken pox. Bill remarked that he felt like a startled deer trying to cross a New York freeway in the middle of rush hour. We were back in the modern world.

The Singapore experience was regular shopping excursions into the city with Katharine. The frequency of our shopping was so embarrassing that Katharine and I couldn't use the "s" word in front of our husbands any longer. It became necessary to refer to our outings as "hiking." But the husbands caught on quickly. Still, Singapore was the first country outside the U.S. where we were able to find American food products. All the food products that we take for granted at home and didn't know we would miss until we didn't have them. Important things like M & M's, Grape Nuts, cottage cheese and cranberry juice. Filling *Pegaso* to the brim with provisions, we headed for Phuket, island of Thailand.

Our son, Burtt and his fiancée, Lisa, joined us there in Patong Beach. We cruised to a few of the out islands and spent Christmas at Phi Phi Island.

Catering to mostly European tourists, yet still charming, there are no roads or motor vehicles on the island, only sandy paths. Along these paths are little huts of combination homes and businesses.

Lisa and I luxuriated in one of these little one-room homes with a Siamese massage on a padded mat. As the wife fixed dinner, the mother-in-law watched TV on the floor beside us, and the baby and dog climbed over our feet, Lisa and I took turns having a massage. Five dollars an hour. In bathing suits, I might add. In the meantime, Burtt was earning his certification in scuba and he and Bill celebrated with a deep-water dive.

In Phuket, the restaurants were numerous along the beach. If you tired of Thai food, you could always get pizza or hamburgers. But the local market sold more interesting fare. Huge barrels filled with small wriggling eels, frogs, turtles and large fried palmetto bugs caught my attention. But never tempted me enough to try them.

Thailand was one of the few places that, as far as we knew, there were no thefts among the yachts. Nothing disappeared from the decks and the dinghies were always safe on the beach. While one yachtie was shopping, the tide carried his dinghy out to sea and a local fisherman struggled to rescue it and find its owner.

Six weeks later, we sailed out of Patong Beach. With a brilliant sunset ahead and the moon already rising behind us, we headed due west for Sri Lanka.

What was a smooth ocean passage for us would be a horror for *First Lady*. Halfway between Thailand and Sri Lanka, in the middle of the ocean, Ned and Jeanette discovered that they were taking on water. Having to pump by hand, the water continued to rise and they could not discover the source of the problem. Richard and Pamela on *Alice Grace* picked up their mayday and relayed it to the fleet. Even though they were the closest boat to *First Lady, Alice Grace* was still upwind and sixty miles away. We were the next closest boat, but one hundred seventy miles away and downwind. It was hard to estimate who would be able to reach her first. We were the faster yacht with the wind in our favor, but further away. They were smaller and, therefore, slower and would have to turn around and tack sixty miles upwind. We only knew there wasn't much time left.

Pegaso and *Alice Grace* changed course and made way toward *First Lady's* last known position. Before losing power, *First Lady's* last report was they were bow down and sinking fast. There was little chance that anyone would find them without radio contact. It would take a miracle.

And a miracle did happen. *Alice Grace* arrived at the very last moment of the window of opportunity to rescue the sinking couple and a few of their belongings. As the four sailors stood on the deck of *Alice Grace* and watched, *First Lady* with the sails still raised, dipped her bow and sailed to the depths of the ocean.

But the drama didn't end there. Once they were safely aboard *Alice Grace*, a "War of the Roses" broke out between the rescued couple. The dispute apparently was the continuation of an ongoing battle. The two combatants were separated and kept apart, a task not easy to perform in such tight quarters as a sailing vessel. The anger was intense and the animosity mounted.

Our involvement did not end with the sinking of *First Lady*. At some point following the initial rescue, the warring wife decided she had enough and jumped overboard about five miles from shore. Since attempting suicide is a serious crime in Sri Lanka, this little piece of information had to be concealed and the incident was reported as an accidental man overboard. That would eventually prompt stern reprimands from maritime officials for our friends aboard *Alice Grace*, causing them considerable anxiety and grief.

In any case, before there was a chance to re-plot our course, we were called upon to continue in a new search and rescue effort for "the body." We searched for hours. Finally, a local fisherman found Jeanette afloat and took her ashore, unscathed.

After a land tour of Sri Lanka, we added a few provisions and set sail for the Maldives. It was here that we needed to make a decision. Were we going to go south around the tip of South Africa or would we go up the Red Sea and into the Mediterranean? It was a unanimous vote. We were headed for the Med.

In the Maldives, we dived and rested in preparation for the sail to Oman, our first stop before heading up the Red Sea. The nine-day sail across the Indian Ocean was the best offshore sail of our entire trip. The seas were calm and glassy. The winds were steady and fair. We were doing seven knots and I couldn't even tell we were underway. It was that comfortable. The hatches were open the entire trip. This is the type of sailing my dreams are made of.

It was Ramadan when we arrived in Oman. The restaurants were closed during the day and we were not allowed on shore after dark. In respect to their customs, I tried to dress as modestly as possible. I put on a skirt that fell just above my ankles, a long-sleeved shirt and a scarf tied under my chin. It was the first time in my life that I was embarrassed that my ankles showed. Still I received harassment from a few of the older Oman men when Bill was not by my side. One old man followed me into the market and jabbed me in the back with his walking stick. Thinking that I was standing in his way, I moved. When I did, he followed after me and jabbed me again. It was then I realized that I was the object of his derision. A white woman, improperly dressed, without an escort. In his eyes I had to be a woman of ill repute. Rather than making me angry, I was saddened and filled with compassion. Compassion for all those who had ever been hated merely because their skin or hair was not the right color. Compassion for the one doing the hating because the hatred will destroy his own spirit. I realized that wherever you are people will separate you into two categories: L.U. or N.L.U.—Like Us or Not Like Us. And that prejudice is everywhere, no matter what country.

From Oman we sailed straight to Djibouti, located at the southern end of the Red Sea. We stayed as far as possible from the coast of Somalia because of the fierce warnings of piracy by that country. It was going to be a six-week journey to get to the top of the Red Sea. Depending on the prevailing political situation between the neighboring countries, it could be a dangerous journey. There was a foreboding feeling among the fifty or so boats that were preparing to sail to the Suez Canal. Knowing all too well that there was safety in numbers, we stuck pretty close to each other as we proceeded north.

Our journey up the Red Sea continued with Jim and Sue Chambers aboard *Sea Shanty* from Wilton, Connecticut. Bill spent part of his childhood in Wilton. Our first meeting with this excellent couple was back in New Caledonia. We met Jim and Sue in different ports along the way and were looking forward to spending more time with them cruising in convoy.

Because of the ever-present southbound winds, there was a lot of stop and go if you were headed north by sailboat. The stopping was to wait until the winds subsided. The going was as far as you were able when it was still. Always under power is how we did it. Some sailors choose to tack from shore to shore, but with big freighters also in the area it can be dangerous.

One of our first stops was Port Smith, a tiny, flat, sandy island with nothing but scrub brush. At first it looked deserted, but in fact five goatherds, many goats and a few camels lived there.

The goatherd stood on the rock that jutted from the island, the closest point he could possibly get to our anchored yachts. Dressed in a long robe, he held in his hand a wooden staff. Persistently, he whistled and called to the two yachts. Conferring by radio with *Sea Shanty*, it was decided that we would venture to shore together to see what he wanted. The young man spoke adequate English and told us that he hadn't seen his master for two weeks. They were out of provisions and they needed food and "white powder" to make bread. Returning to the yachts, we gathered flour, canned sardines and a few other items to leave with the young goatherds.

Mits'iwa in Eritrea was our next brief stop. The recent civil war left its mark. Bombed out buildings and derelict armor tanks formed the scenery. The people were friendly and curious about the few rare visitors. American dollars were very desired.

Most vivid in my memory of the Red Sea is Suakin in Sudan. The first sight one sees when entering the port is a city in ruins. This skeleton city was once the main port. When the port was moved to Port Sudan, the people followed where the commerce would take them. As the economy deteriorated in Suakin, those who remained behind removed timber from the vacated buildings for cooking. Like the Biblical Jericho, the walls came tumbling down leaving nothing but crumbled ruins. A few still live among the ruins.

This is where Taj lives, an affectionate, bright, ebullient boy. Taj quickly and easily worked his way into my heart and is still there. He spoke excellent English and elected himself our official host inviting us to his home for tea with the poise of a grown man. Walking through the ruins, it was hard to believe that anyone could live in such a manner. His father welcomed us into his home but was visibly perturbed that Taj was bringing strangers for tea. Father returned to his daily prayer ritual while Taj prepared tea over a tiny fire in the middle of the decaying surroundings. With dignity, Taj poured very carefully so as not to spill one drop and sitting cross-legged on the bare ground, we sipped our tea.

After, Taj took us by the hand and guided us to the local market. As we bartered with the local vendors for produce and bread, he made sure we got the best deal possible. Other little children joined us but Taj made sure they understood we belonged to him.

"Watch out for him," Taj said. Warning us about another boy about twelve years old. "He's no good. He's a bully. He doesn't go to school and he smokes. He's a stupid boy."

After we left Suakin, I couldn't get Taj out of my thoughts. There was something special about this child. If he were living somewhere else, there might be a chance for him and others like him. But in war-torn Sudan? We left Taj standing on the shore watching us leave, and with tears in my eyes, I knew we had a freedom from strife he would never know.

In all our travels, no area affected me like Sudan. In many countries, we had seen poor areas, but there was peace. We saw need, but there was joy. But never had we seen such despair as here.

Sea Shanty and *Pegaso* sat anchored for four days in Marsa abu Imama. The winds were so strong that it was impossible to take the dinghy from our boat to theirs. On shore, there was nothingness. Only desert and an occasional camel train. And so we waited out the tempest weather.

Finally, the winds died and we picked up to leave. With the sun in our faces, it was impossible to see the shallow reef to maneuver around it. I went forward to the bow to get a better view. Directing Bill as he steered, I pointed him in the wrong direction and toward the reef. Thank goodness, he knew better. Bill remembered where the reef was and maneuvered *Pegaso* safely out through the pass.

Ballentine wasn't as fortunate, however. A short time before, Herb and his daughter, Lynn, were in the same marsa or cove. They did hit the reef and it broke their rudder. This began a real tale of woe for them. They were able to re-anchor, dinghy to shore and hitch a ride to Port Sudan in the back of an open-bed truck with seven Sudanese men. When the truck broke down, Herb and Lynn spent the night in the desert in the back of the truck. The Sudanese managed to get the truck running again the following morning and they continued on their way.

The best they could do when they returned to their boat was to jury-rig the rudder, but they needed more manpower to get to Port Suez. Taking on two of the Sudanese as extra crew, they left for the next port, Safaga. A short time later, the rudder broke again and they were unable to steer.

Via radio, they were able to arrange a tow to Safaga just a few miles away. The tow company turned out to be the Egyptian Navy.

After *Ballentine* was safely in port, the captain presented them with a bill for $28,500. Herb protested the excessive charge, but still the military wouldn't budge. While they argued the fee, Herb repaired the rudder and was ready to leave. But the Egyptian Navy refused to allow Herb to leave and demanded that he sign a check made out in Arabic. Realizing that his bank probably would not honor such a document, Herb tried to explain this. The stubborn officials would not budge. The two Sudanese on board did not help matters any because Egypt was at war with Sudan. So, Herb obliged them, signed the document and correctly assumed that he better get to the Mediterranean as quickly as possible.

One week later, an Egyptian gunboat caught up with Herb and Lynn in Hurgada. Advancing rapidly with guns aimed toward *Ballentine,* they placed an armed guard on board. They accused Herb of giving them a bad check and forced *Ballentine* to return to Safaga.

The boat was chained to the wharf and assigned two armed guards to stand watch twenty-four hours a day. At first, they were not allowed to leave the boat, but eventually they were able to convince authorities they would not abandon the boat and skip the country.

It was at this point that we met Herb and Lynn and heard them tell of their exploit in a Safaga restaurant.

The saga could have gone on for months or years if they decided to fight the fine in the courts of Egypt. Even then, in all likelihood, the courts would have upheld the demands of their own Navy against foreigners. Within a couple of weeks, the Navy had its payment and *Ballentine* couldn't get out of the Red Sea fast enough.

Herb and Lynn made it back to Jamestown, Rhode Island safe and sound. The adventure didn't dampen their spirits any. *Ballentine* spends the winters in the Caribbean. I assume she is happier there.

In spite of certain unpleasant memories in Egypt, that area of the Red Sea is a diver's paradise. Several hotels overlook crystal clear water that attracts scuba buffs from around the world. It's easy to see why. The Red Sea has, to me anyway, the best diving in the world.

Passage through the Suez Canal was simple since there were no locks. Dropping the sails and motoring the channel proved to be a smooth jaunt that lasted two days, anchoring overnight in the canal. We were warned by the guidebook that this was an area to watch out for, so Bill was alert during our overnight anchorage. Sure enough, when he investigated strange noises on deck in the middle of the night, our lines had been cut and the ropes stolen along with a small extra anchor.

Dealing with customs and immigration officials is usually tedious but not painful. It is true that they have the authority to arrest you and impound your boat for any reason they want. But we never felt that any official would abuse this privilege. Except in Egypt.

The minute we passed through the canal exit and into the Mediterranean, we breathed a sigh of relief. It was liberating to leave that part of the world behind.

15

The Mediterranean and Homeward Bound

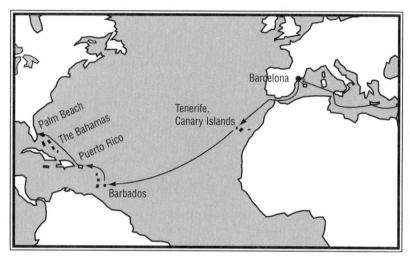

On the radio, friends in Cyprus were telling us, "When you get here, you'll think you've died and gone to heaven."

Well, I wouldn't exactly say that. But after spending the last 10,000 miles pushing to get to the Mediterranean, it certainly was a relief. The past year was an adventure. A trip back into history. A strange mixture of Biblical times and present day. But it was exhausting, too.

Cyprus was a good place to stop, rest and make another decision. Bill was thinking of going back to school. Yes, school. Ever since we left home, he was studying. History, chemistry, physics, economics—any kind of educational book he could find to read along the way. It was in Cyprus that Bill made the decision to enter the Executive Master's Program in Business Administration at the University of Chicago in Barcelona. He was accepted and we had six weeks to sail 2,800 miles across the Mediterranean Sea to Spain. Stopping briefly in the Greek islands, Sicily, Sardinia, and Malta, we arrived in Barcelona, our home for the next year.

Life changed dramatically for us at this point. Instead of moving constantly from anchorage to anchorage, we were now cozily tied to the wharf in Puerto Olimpico at the foot of the city. Instead of wearing shorts and T-shirts and arriving for dinner with bare feet-now we needed to dress for the big city. Instead of English-speaking yachties for friends, we made a whole new set of friends among the Catalan/Spanish speaking locals.

Barcelona. I can't say enough about this wonderful city. The people, the architecture, the lifestyle. We loved it. It took no time at all to feel right at home. The people come in all sizes and colors-blondes and brunettes, blue eyes and brown eyes, tall and short. After I bought a few city clothes, I could be mistaken for one of them. It always pleased me when someone would approach me on a street corner and ask for directions in Catalan. I would answer in Spanish that I could help them with the directions but that I couldn't speak Catalan. I loved the look on their faces when they realized I was a foreigner.

It was surprising to discover that the first language in Barcelona is not Spanish but Catalan. Thinking we were going to improve our Spanish, that endeavor turned out to be more difficult than expected. Barcelona is in an autonomous region of Spain called Catalonia. The people are very proud of their Catalonian roots and reluctantly speak Spanish to anyone except tourists. If someone from Madrid should come to Barcelona he would be given the cold shoulder if he did not speak Catalan, and most likely he couldn't.

Our local friends would say, "The Americans are here. We must speak Spanish." The conversation would start out fine for us and we would understand almost everything that was said. Shortly, they would just naturally revert back to speaking Catalan and Bill and I would be left out of the conversation until they saw the perplexed looks on our faces.

Thanks to Bill's love for tennis, we made many friends very quickly by joining the Royal Tennis Club of Barcelona where all the top Spanish professionals belong. Arantxa Sanchez-Vicario, Carlos Moya, Carlos and Alberto Costa, and others regularly practice there. Bill played almost every day.

Instead of a car or mopeds, we bought bicycles because parking would be simpler. I enrolled at the University of Barcelona in a Spanish class for foreigners. Every day I would bicycle several miles through the busy streets to school, then get groceries, visit museums, or shop on Paseo de Gracia. In the open market, the customer is not allowed to pick his own fruit. The vendor does it for you. At first, I was given the bruised produce because I was *extranjera* or a foreigner. But my new friend, Rosalia, took me under her wing and introduced me to her vendor-friends with instructions that I was to get the best.

Rosalia Martiń and her husband, Eduardo, owned the shop where we bought our bicycles. They opened their hearts and their home to us above and beyond all our expectations during our stay in Barcelona.

The families nicknamed us *las gallinas*, the chickens, or in this case the early birds, because we went to bed so early. Dinner at the Martiń home began at 10:30 and during holidays we would join the neighborhood in the streets for dancing until the wee hours of the morning. Trying to keep up with them was futile. We would excuse ourselves at what we thought was a respectable hour—around two in the morning—to go home to bed. The amused look on their faces was memorable, as they would say, "There go the early birds."

Rosalia was very patient with my Spanish and would repeat the same point over and over until I understood her perfectly. Her dark eyes would sparkle when she shared little tidbits of gossip. As we walked down the street, she would wrap her arm tightly in mine and whisper in my ear about the neighbors. "That man is very rich. He owns the big factory on the corner. That woman makes tricky-tricky with the butcher," and on and on. She was a fountain of information about everyone that we passed.

Rosalia was born in the same room and even in the same bed, that she and her husband were now sleeping. Three generations—the grandparents, Ramoń and Agueda, Rosalia and Eduardo and their twenty-five-year old daughter, Monica were living in the same tiny apartment on the third floor of a five-story walkup. The rooms were so small that they probably had no more square footage than we had on our boat. It was packed with knick-knacks and memorabilia from the sixty-some years of living there. Once we were seated at their dining table, it was impossible to move until dinner was over.

Papa, as we called him, was eighty-nine, sweet and gentle spoken. His hair was thick and white and still covered his whole head. He moved slowly but could think rapidly. Ramoń with a little prodding would tell us stories at dinner. He recounted how Franco made a law against speaking, reading or writing their native Catalan language. The punishment was imprisonment and possibly death. The people were even afraid to speak the language in the privacy of their homes. This probably accounts for the reason that the Catalans so adamantly want to preserve their heritage to this day.

Ramoń was born in the pueblo of El Tormo. This tiny mountain village dates back 400 years with homes that share common walls. The streets are only able to accommodate two horses passing or one compact car at a time. With a year-round population of two hundred, the tiny town swells to about a thousand inhabitants returning to their hometown for fiesta in August. It was a rare opportunity to be able to visit this picturesque village. Tourists have not discovered it because there are no hotels. Even most Spaniards have never heard of El Tormo.

The home in which Ramoń was born has been in his family for over two hundred years. We were his guests in this beautiful rustic structure for a weekend of celebrations. The structure has three narrow floors and shares its walls in townhouse style. The ground floor is made up of a living room and kitchen. The second floor is one master bedroom and the top floor is an attic that was converted into a bath and more beds.   Rosalia and the family were very apologetic that it was "so humble and ugly." Touched by the hospitality shown us, we assured them that we were perfectly comfortable,

On the first night of the festivities, everyone from babies to grand parents danced to music on the loudspeaker in the center of the town until four in the morning. Everyone except Bill and me. About one o'clock we excused ourselves from the festivities and went to bed. But not to sleep. After the music stopped, the villagers remained to chat until the sun came up. The church clock directly outside our bedroom window rang faithfully all night long every half-hour. It also rang once five minutes before each chime to announce that it was going to chime. We certainly didn't have to guess what time it was. Edgar Allan Poe must have visited there and used the experience as inspiration to write his poem about the bells, the bells, bells, bells.

The following day we passed time waiting for the big moment happening at midnight, the running of the bulls. In preparation, bulls were brought from the countryside in trucks. The men managed to maneuver the trucks through the narrow streets and carefully back the vehicles tightly against the opening of the corral. Men perched on the top of the truck raised the back door and began to jab the bulls to drive them into the corral. The truck shook and lurched as the bulls fought against the steel prods. Blood and caca flew in all directions and we quickly backed away. At last, the bulls burst into the arena to wait, like us, for the excitement to begin.

Tension mounted as the townspeople prepared their homes. Steel rods and tree trunks were secured across open doorways to keep the bulls from charging into someone's living room as they stampeded through the streets. At 10:30 in the evening, we sat outside at the table for a dinner of cheese, bread, olives, dried and salted pork and red wine.

After dinner, everyone gathered in the doorways behind their homemade barricades and on the balconies to watch the lighting of the bull's horns. The task took approximately seventy-five young men on two ropes. They struggled to pull the bull a mere 50 feet from the corral to a stake in the middle of the road. He snorted and bellowed and dug his heels in. He tugged against the ropes and tried in vain to find soft flesh with his horns. He fought fiercely but the men succeeded in tying his head and placed a flaming torch at the end of each horn. Each man stood his ground until the bull was released for fear that someone would think him cowardly. As soon as the bull was free, the men made a quick dash for safety. The bull, confused and frightened, ran through the streets in a wild frenzy. To impress their sweethearts and wives, the men would tease and prod the bulls into charging and then run for cover while the crowd cheered them on. As the bull regained his senses, he became fiercer and the young men became less macho. There didn't seem to be any real reason for any of it except to provide entertainment at the expense of one confused and angry bull.

Nevertheless, we are grateful to Ramón and his family for taking us into their hearts and home and introducing us to this experience of the true Old Spain.

Summertime in Barcelona is hot and humid. But as winter promised to be colder than we wanted it to be, Bill and I decided it would be a good time to visit our mothers in Palm Beach.

Renting a house there for the winter months, we flew home to see the family. All the children and grandchildren came to visit and we enjoyed the time together. In fact, we liked it so much that one rainy afternoon when we didn't have anything better to do, we bought a house. It wasn't really that simple. Nevertheless, we often had conversations about where we wanted to settle down and finally made a decision.

After our vacation in Palm Beach was over, we returned to *Pegaso* in Barcelona. Bill was still going to school, but now we looked forward to sailing to our new home in Florida. However, two more years would pass before we would finally sail into the port of Palm Beach.

For the time being, we would enjoy skiing in France and touring Italy, Portugal and the rest of Spain. After our "holiday away from our vacation"— as we referred to it—ended, we drove out of France, south down the coast of Portugal and circled back up through Spain. Entering the mountain areas of the Spanish interior, we ran into a snowstorm and decided to spend the night. We spotted a reasonably attractive building with a "hotel" sign on it. Bill was suspicious of the quality of the hotel because it didn't have any rating stars on the sign. But it looked good enough to me. I was tired and I just wanted a warm place to lay my head.

Grabbing our luggage, we hopped out of the car and ran through the falling snow into the lobby. When we walked into the lobby, we saw about twenty-five lovely young ladies lined up at a bar. All heads turned towards us when we entered. Bill took me by the arm and said, "Let's get out of here." Cold and tired, I said, "Why? I'm tired. I want to stay." As Bill tugged on my arm, he whispered in my ear. "Because it's a brothel." Stubbornly I resisted, "It can't be. It says 'hotel'."

Cat calls and laughter rang in our ears as Bill dragged me out. And I thought our adventures were over?

The time came to leave Barcelona. With it came the same sadness at saying goodbye to new friends mixed with excitement of what lay ahead.

After stops on Mallorca and Ibiza, we day-tripped our way down through the Straits of Gibraltar into the Atlantic, and then set a southerly course for the Canary Islands.

The Canaries are a popular jumping off spot for many transatlantic sailors. We stayed for a month at Tenerife with about fifteen other boats One by one, we tossed off the lines of our fellow cruisers as we wished them well on their passage. After stocking the freezer and tending to maintenance, it was time for us to cast off. It would be our final long passage—and it would not be trouble-free.

The sour memories of our first Atlantic passage seven years earlier hadn't left me. The seasickness was gone, as was the fear of the unknown. But now I was plagued with a different fear—a fear of the known. I was now a seasoned sailor and knew the most dangerous part of the trip lay just ahead.

We began our Atlantic crossing on December 20, 1996. The weather was pleasant. Bill set the sails and turned on the autopilot. The wind was behind us and we went forward to pole out the jib and sail wing on wing—the forward jib set in the opposite direction of the main.

With luck, the wind would keep us on a steady course to our destination—Barbados.

There is a boater's rhyme about the weather that goes "Red sky at night, sailor's delight. Red sky at morn, sailors be warned." Several days later, we awoke to a red sky. The winds were already kicking up and the seas were becoming confused. The waves were not frighteningly high—only about six feet—but they were beating us up from every direction. One would hit from the port side and the next would hit on the starboard side, tossing *Pegaso* back and forth like a lone sneaker in a washing machine. We weren't in any danger but the constant jerking motion wears on the nerves. When a sailor becomes irritable and testy, that's when he—or in this case, she—makes critical mistakes. What happened next was no one's fault, just one of those things.

Without warning our previously dependable autopilot decided we should be going in the opposite direction. As we took a sharp left turn, the wind grabbed the sails and flipped us sideways, snapping the spinnaker pole in two and twisting it into the main sail, ripping it down the middle.

Bill turned off the autopilot and grabbed the helm to correct our course. There was no response.

"We don't have any steering," said Bill. "I'll have to empty the aft storage and see what's wrong."

Our challenges now were to repair the steering and the sail. Even I knew that without these, we were in serious trouble.

We dropped the sails and with no forward movement, we bobbed around like a cork. I helped Bill unload the "garage" while he dug down to the rudder.

"Everything is okay here," he said. "I'll check the hydraulics."

Bill found it. "A small leak in the hydraulic system allowed air bubbles into the steering. Some more fluid should fix it for now," he said.

Next it was time to repair the sail. We were still tossing about as we put on our safety harnesses and tied ourselves to the mast facing one another.

"You stand on that side and pass the needle through to me," Bill said.

As I pushed hard with the steel palm glove, the needle slowly passed through the heavy sail. Bill grabbed the needle and pulled it to his side and repeated the same motion. We kept sewing as a team. I stopped for a moment to look around and absorb the situation. Here we were just a tiny dot in the middle of the ocean. There was no drama. It was just another day, in another passage, with another chore that needed doing.

We celebrated the holidays in the middle of the Atlantic Ocean. On Christmas Eve, we sat in the cockpit and looked up at the sky. It was the most beautiful sunset I had ever seen. God lit up the sky with radiant pillows of fluffy pink clouds that He hung with puffs of magenta and orange. The scene so resembled a Christmas tree that it took my breath away.

It was a time to give Him thanks for all His blessings. For bringing us this far, healthy and safe. For watching over our family. For the kind, wonderful husband He sent me. For the bonding we gained from our experience together. For how far He brought me since my initial plea when I wrote my prayer.

Eighteen days and 2,800 miles after leaving Tenerife, we made landfall in Barbados. We were back in the Caribbean.

Things had changed. The natives seemed friendlier. Or did we change? Was our outlook on life so different than when we began our trip seven years ago? Of course it was.

We were no longer living life in the fast lane. If our needs weren't met immediately, it could wait until tomorrow. If someone stole our dinghy motor, well, maybe he needed it worse than we did. At least he was nice enough to leave us the oars. So what if we couldn't get our favorite cereal. We'd eat bananas instead. We didn't get news from the United States and we didn't want it. They only report the bad news anyway. We gladly missed the whole O.J. Simpson trial. We missed the detailed coverage of the Oklahoma City bombing. It was good to live in Utopia. And I never had to read a single tedious list of "what's in" and "what's out" in American society.

I tried to unwind and just enjoy what the next five months would bring as we headed home through the Caribbean and Bahamas. We sailed north, stopping at many of the same islands as before—Bequia, St. Lucia, Martinique, Dominica, Antigua, St. Barts—eager to find some of the same boat boys who had befriended us or eat at some of the same memorable restaurants.

When we reached Bequia our circumnavigation was legitimate. Even though we began our trip twice—first from Sandusky in *Alicia* and again in *Pegaso* from Ft. Lauderdale—we crossed our path in Bequia. Officially, we were completed. But our goal was West Palm Beach. Only twelve hundred miles to go.

We stopped in Dominica and were welcomed again by Raymond, now a married man with children. Replacing his dilapidated windsurfer, he had graduated to a sharp little skiff with a big fancy motor. We gave Raymond a photo taken of him on our previous visit. He gave us a toothy smile and promised he remembered when we were there seven years ago. We inquired about the Swiss chef who had prepared one of our most memorable meals. "Sorry. You are too late. He died one week ago."

As we got closer to the Bahamas, the problem with the steering dogged us yet again. Now that we were sailing between islands and closer to land in shallower waters, the glitch in the hydraulics was more than an annoyance. It was dangerous.

Now that I knew all the things that could go wrong, I caught a bad case of the what-ifs. What if we are going through a narrow passage and the steering fails again—in the Bahamas with a shallow reef on both sides? Worse than that. What if we are going through the Lake Worth Inlet—just minutes from home—and the boat decides to make a sharp left turn into the jetty? Then we would crash and have to be rescued in our own hometown. What a horrible homecoming that would be. How embarrassing. I could see the headline: "Couple Wrecks Boat Moments Before Completing Around the World Cruise." I drove Bill nuts.

As we leisurely worked our way up the Bahama Islands chain, something happened that convinced Bill I needed a break from cruising.

After a day's passage, we dropped the anchor in a lovely spot at a deserted island. We went for a snorkel, then had dinner in the cockpit and watched the sunset. I decided to take a look at the chart to see where we were and immediately became upset.

"Bill, we're in that same spot where those two men boarded us seven years ago."

"Uh huh," he said.

"Did you know that?"

"Mmm," he said.

"I don't want to be here."

"It's dark and it's too late to move."

"But, what if….."

"It's all right. We'll lock up tightly tonight. Everything will be okay."

"But, what if….."

"We'll be fine."

My mind drifted back to that day when we returned to *Pegaso* from our snorkel at this very same anchorage and discovered those strangers on board. The men were polite and left. But that was then and then I was ignorant. I didn't know all the things that could go wrong. Now I was a coward—but an educated coward—and my imagination was working overtime.

I was a nervous wreck and slept fitfully. At midnight, the noise of the bilge pump awakened me and I sat straight up in bed. I should have recognized the sound right away after spending two thousand five hundred days listening to the bilge pump intermittently empty water overboard. Instead, I thought someone was sneaking up on us and jabbed Bill in the ribs.

"I just heard an engine go off," I said. "Someone's here. Get the gun."

It was the first time that we felt a need to retrieve the pistol from its hiding place in the engine room. It was still wrapped in tin foil, in a plastic container, hidden among the spare parts.

Bill sprung out of bed, making as much noise as possible to scare the "intruders."

We didn't turn on the lights for fear that we would make ourselves a better target. We crouched on deck peering into the blackness of the night, trying to spot any sign of a boat or bandit. That was when we remembered that the dinghy was still tied to the stern.

"Let's bring the dinghy up."

We had performed this job hundreds of times before—but not in total darkness. And not with my adrenaline overriding my brain. Bill climbed overboard and got into the dinghy. I unlatched one end of the mizzen halyard and handed it to Bill—forgetting that I had already unwound the other end. The halyard went flying out of the mast and hit the water with a loud splash. I envisioned an intruder jumping overboard.

"There he goes." I began screaming. Short, high yips. "Eee, Eee, Eee."

By now, I had worked my knight in shining armor into believing what my overactive imagination had invented.

"I've got a gun, you (censored). You'd better get off now." As Bill continued to shout into the dark, I realized what had happened. Now I had to confess.

"Bill….uh, Bill, Honey," I said. "It was the halyard. The halyard. It's in the water." My voice started to rise apologetically.

"The halyard."

"Uh, yes. That's what made that big splash."

There was silence. I could tell that he was thinking this one over.

"Promise me you won't tell anyone this story," he said.

"I promise."

I kept that promise until now.

The rest of the trip was peaceful. With one last short overnight passage from Eleuthera we crossed the Gulf Stream and sailed safely through the Lake Worth Inlet on Mother's Day, 1997. We tied *Pegaso* to the dock in West Palm Beach at Rybovich-Spencer Marina. Two hours later we moved into our new house.

Bill's dream came true. We did it. We sailed around the world. Just the two of us.

And all we needed were the wings of a prayer.

From the Captain

As captain, I always felt responsible for our safety and comfort at sea, especially Alicia's. I felt a moral obligation to Alicia because she had no sailing experience and had come on the trip primarily to please me. When we left port for a trip of a thousand miles or more, I always felt some apprehension about what would happen. The level of apprehension was based on the trip. For example, sailing back and forth to New Zealand from Tonga and Fiji can be dangerous because of strong storms, and I worried a lot. I worried about pirates when sailing through parts of Indonesia. I always tried to appear confident and relaxed to Alicia so she wouldn't worry. During a voyage in an area with the potential for violent weather, I would anxiously await weather news. It wasn't until we were crossing the Atlantic at the end of our trip that I decided not to worry. The trip had lots of little problems, but once I decided the weather was in God's hands, I relaxed and let Him worry about it. And when I finally decided that my fate was in God's hands is when I, too, turned my life over to Him and became a believer.

Bill Blodgett

Photo Montage

On board *Alicia* in the Caribbean.

A typical day. That's *Pegaso* in the background.

Bill and guide, Miguel, cooking chicken on a stick in the Venezuelan jungle.

Alicia transits the Panama Canal.

Pass extended on same

22 NOV 199

Edwino brings us dinner in the San Blas.

Cuna Indian of the San Blas Islands displays
her molas for sale.

Bill—A quick dip in the cool tropical paradise of Rarotonga.

Sea lions share their beach with us in the Galapagos Islands.

Pass extended on same   22 NOV 199

The church on Palmerston Island built 150 years ago from a shipwreck .

A Tongan feast given in our honor after we donated the short wave radio.

Congratulations! You did it! The bungy champs,
Bill and son, Todd.

The "girls" tandem skydiving in New Zealand with instructors. That's daughter, Shari,
in the middle. Mom, on the far right, flew the plane.

Bill and son, Burtt in Auckland, New Zealand.

A common sight—dolphins following *Pegaso*.

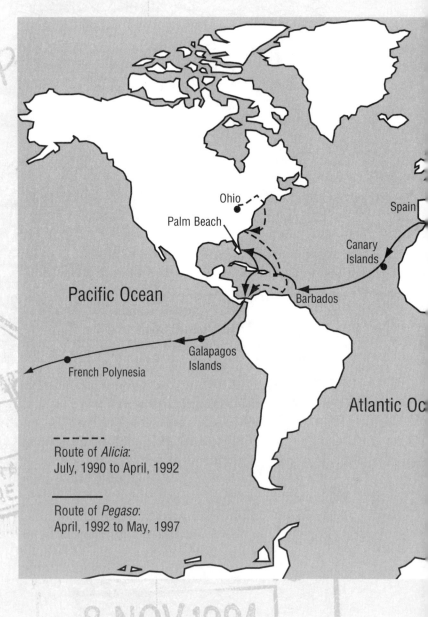

Ohio

Palm Beach

Spain

Canary
Islands

Pacific Ocean

Barbados

French Polynesia

Galapagos
Islands

Atlantic Oc

- - - - - -
Route of *Alicia*:
July, 1990 to April, 1992

Route of *Pegaso*:
April, 1992 to May, 1997

- 8 NOV 1994

Pass extended on same

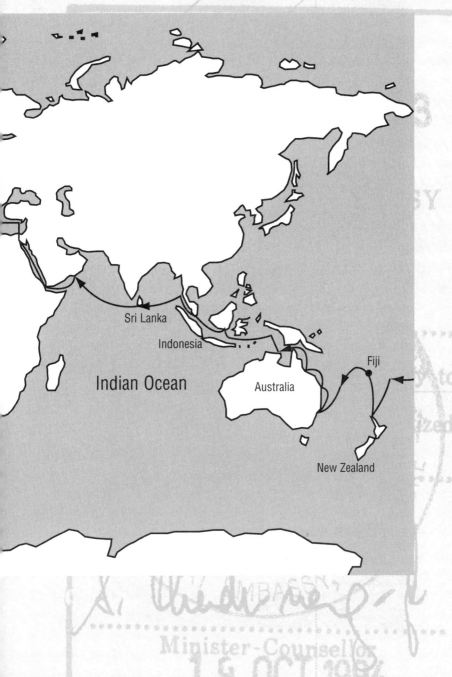

Bill and friends in Vanuatu.

Moorea, 1992.

Fiji—Even though *Pegaso* had a washer and dryer, I enjoyed washing our clothes in the river with the ladies.

Introducing our Fijian friends to popcorn. Left to right: Jane Lucid, Lusi, Semi and their daughters, Morgan Lucid, and Bill.

In Vanuatu, these villagers posed for five U.S. dollars contributed to the chief, far right.

Excited islanders come out to greet the "fleet" on Baubau in Indonesia.

Indonesian weaving fabric in the shade of her stilt home. I bought the black and silver piece by her side.

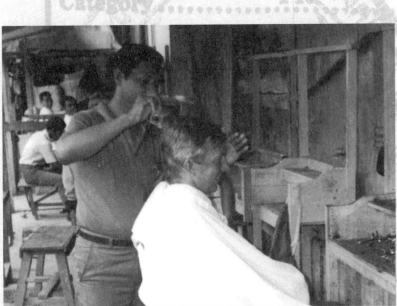

Bill gets a haircut on the street in Indonesia.

Dentistry on the sidewalk in Indonesia. A patient inspects his recently extracted molar.

Suakin, Sudan. The little boy on the right is the unforgettable Taj.

Pegaso —The cockpit provided good protection from the elements.

The spacious galley including full-size oven, microwave, toaster oven and triple sinks.

The salon table that seats ten provided plenty of room for entertaining.

The comfortable master stateroom. I took one look at the large bed and storage space and knew *Pegaso* was me.